Contact
U.S.A.

Paul Abraham
Bradford College

Daphne Mackey
University of Washington

Second Edition

Contact
U.S.A.

Reading and Vocabulary Textbook

Illustrated by Marci Davis

PRENTICE HALL REGENTS
Englewood Cliffs, New Jersey 07632

Library of Congress Cataloging-in-Publication Data

Abraham, Paul
    Contact U.S.A. : reading and vocabulary textbook / Paul Abraham,
Daphne Mackey ; illustrated by Marci Davis.
        p.   cm.
    ISBN 0-13-169616-5
    1. English language--Textbooks for foreign speakers.   I. Mackey,
Daphne. II. Title. III. Title: Contact USA.
PE1128.A27 1989
428.2'4--dc19   88-25565
                                                          CIP

Editorial/production supervision: Linda Zuk
Cover design: Wanda Lubelska Design
Manufacturing buyer: Laura Crossland

© 1989, 1982 by Prentice Hall Regents
Prentice-Hall, Inc.
A Paramount Communications Company
Englewood Cliffs, New Jersey 07632

Printed in the United States of America
16 15 14 13 12 11

ISBN 0-13-169616-5

Prentice-Hall International (UK) Limited, *London*
Prentice-Hall of Australia Pty. Limited, *Sydney*
Prentice-Hall Canada Inc., *Toronto*
Prentice-Hall Hispanoamericana, S.A., *Mexico*
Prentice-Hall of India Private Limited, *New Delhi*
Prentice-Hall of Japan, Inc., *Tokyo*
Simon & Schuster Asia Pte. Ltd., *Singapore*
Editora Prentice-Hall do Brasil, Ltda., *Rio de Janeiro*

To the unsung professionals of ESL

Contents

Acknowledgments

Many people have given us feedback and suggestions that have helped us in revising *Contact U.S.A.* We would especially like to thank Chérie Lenz-Hackett and Fredricka Stoller for their enthusiasm for *Contact U.S.A.* and for their work in reviewing our ideas for this revision. In addition, we thank Chérie for lending us her files and for letting us use her student surveys, several of which are included here in the background building exercises.

Our thanks also to Rachel Goodman, Carol Pineiro, Linda Miller, and Cheryl Rivkin in Boston, and Kathryn Allahyari, Sandy Silberstein, Bruce McCutcheon, Aaron Bidelspach, Patty Heiser, Linda Williams, Becky Boon, and Kimberly Newcomer at the University of Washington. We appreciate their interest in this revision and their suggestions.

Introduction to the Teacher

Contact U.S.A. is a reading and vocabulary text for high-beginning and low-intermediate ESL/EFL students. Although its structure and exercises are aimed primarily at developing academic reading skills and vocabulary, its content (a look at changes in values and lifestyles in the United States) is highly appropriate for all non-native English speakers, including immigrants, students in higher educational institutions, and students of English in foreign countries.

Reading

Reading for high-beginning and low-intermediate students is sometimes a frustrating experience. Books that are appropriate in terms of the students' active English proficiency are often not challenging for adult readers, either in structure or content. Readings that match the student's intellectual or conceptual interest level usually have exercises requiring a more advanced active English proficiency. We have written this book on the premise that adult students at this level of English proficiency are able to read and understand more in English than they are able to produce actively. Therefore, although the readings may appear to be difficult for students at this level at first glance, the first analytical exercises are relatively simple, requiring only passive reading and vocabulary skills. We feel that these types of reading and vocabulary skills are important for students to develop, particularly because the analysis of a reading beyond their proficiency level is a process that students confront in standardized tests in English. The reading exercises in this book progress from main idea to inference. The following is a general outline of each chapter.

Chapter Outline

Section 1: A First Look

A. Background Building

B. Topic (skimming reading for topic of paragraphs)

C. Reading

D. Scanning/Vocabulary (similar-different analysis of vocabulary in the context of the reading)

E. Reading Comprehension (multiple choice)

Section 2: Look Again

A. Vocabulary (multiple choice)

B. Reading Comprehension (cloze summary or outline)

C. Think About It (active comprehension analysis of reading)

D. Reading (graphs or short readings related to the topic—can be used out of sequence in the chapter)

Section 3: Contact a Point of View

A. Background Building

B. Timed Reading (a personal observation followed by True, False, or Impossible to Know statements)

C. Vocabulary

D. React (semi-controlled discussion activities)

E. Word Analysis (Part 1: progressing through the book from recognition of function and form to production of appropriate forms; Part 2: stems and affixes)

Section 4: Look Back

A. Vocabulary (multiple choice)

B. Matching (synonyms)

C. Synthesis Questions (questions for discussion and suggestions for extension activities)

D. Vocabulary Preview

The teacher's guide contains Vocabulary Review Tests and Answer Keys (both for chapter exercises and the review tests).

Vocabulary

This book was written with the firm belief that dictionaries are generally a reading inhibitor rather than a reading enhancer. With this in mind, the cardinal rule of the book is NO DICTIONARIES ALLOWED. The meaning of much of the vocabulary is implied within the reading passage, as the students discover when they complete the first vocabulary exercise, which requires them to analyze words within the context of the reading and compare them to other words that they already know. The vocabulary exercises and the inaccessibility of a dictionary force the students to look for meaning within the context, an essential reading skill. This book serves as a vocabulary builder because we reuse the vocabulary throughout the book so that students are forced to recall vocabulary from previous chapters, where it is used in different contexts. This leads to actual acquisition of the words in the text.

Content

From our experience as teachers, we feel that adult language learners need stimulating reading materials that (1) provide them with background information about American culture, (2) encourage their awareness of their environment, (3) prepare them to deal with the environment of the United States, and (4) let them draw their own conclusions about the United States. The presentation of information about the life and values in the United States is a very touchy subject; students are sensitive to "pro-America" rhetoric. In spite of this wariness, however, students want to understand some of the basic values and issues in the United States. We have chosen themes that have always generated a lot of discussion in class and about which students have strong opinions. The focus of these readings is primarily cross-cultural. The readings enable students and the teacher to examine American culture, to evaluate their feelings, and to redefine their positions in this culture or in their own cultures. We have tried to present, as far as possible, an apolitical portrayal of the United States. The first reading in every chapter is general, giving the overall idea and the key vocabulary items connected to the subject. The timed reading is a personal point of view about some aspect of the subject. For example, the timed reading in the chapter on immigration is from the point of view of a native American. The chapter on race issues has a second reading about reverse discrimination. These points of view are closely tied in with the speaking activities in each chapter, encouraging students to express their ideas about the subject. Since these readings are our personal impressions, and are, as such, debatable, we encourage teachers to feel free to contribute their own personal points of view and to express their cultural perspectives.

Introduction to the Student

Contact U.S.A. has two purposes:

1. to improve your READING ability, and

2. to improve your VOCABULARY.

Each chapter in the book has:

A First Look: exercises to determine general meaning of reading and vocabulary items.

A. Background Building

B. Topic

C. Reading

D. Scanning/Vocabulary (similar/different)

E. Reading Comprehension

Look Again: more detailed exercises in reading comprehension and vocabulary

A. Vocabulary

B. Reading Comprehension

C. React

D. Reading

Contact a Point of View: additional reading:

A. Background Building

B. Timed Reading Exercise

C. Vocabulary

D. React

E. Word Analysis

Look Back: review of the vocabulary from the chapter:

A. Vocabulary

B. Matching

C. Synthesis Questions

D. Vocabulary Preview

The first chapter, "Impressions of the United States," has special instructions for each exercise. These instructions will teach you how to use the book effectively.

Contact
U.S.A.

Impressions
of the United States

A First Look

A. Background Building

1a. What are the first things you think of when you hear the words, "United States?" What words come into your head? Write them here.

> **Example:** (big, crowded streets)

Share your ideas with a classmate.

b. Look at your words again. Are they *positive*, *negative*, or *neutral* (not positive or negative)? Write them again here.

POSITIVE   NEGATIVE   NEUTRAL

                 (crowded streets)   (big)

What were most of your words? Why?

2a. What is in the illustration on page 1? Write the words here.

b. Why are these things in the picture? What other things do you think should be in the picture?

3. What do you want to learn about the United States?

B. Topic

DIRECTIONS: Before you begin to read, look at these topics. There is one topic for each paragraph. Look quickly at the reading to find these topics. Do not read every word at this point. Write the number of the paragraph next to the topic of that paragraph.

1. ___2___ positive and negative ideas about the United States

2. _____ knowledge of a country

3. _____ this book about the United States

4. _____ first thoughts about the United States

5. _____ how people form impressions

C. Reading

DIRECTIONS: Now read, but try to think about groups of words, not individual words. Do not stop if you do not know the meaning of a word.

1 The United States. What is your first thought when you hear *1*
these words? Is it an image of something typically American?* Per- *2*
haps you think of hamburgers and fast-food restaurants. Or per- *3*
haps you have an image of a product, such as an American car or *4*
Coca-Cola®. Some people immediately think of American universi- *5*
ties. Others think of American companies. Many Americans think *6*
of the red, white, and blue flag when they think of the United States. *7*
There are many images associated with the name of a country. *8*

2 There are also many ideas or concepts associated with the *9*
words *United States*. Some people think of a positive concept, such *10*
as freedom, when they think of the United States. Other people *11*
think of a negative concept, such as American involvement in other *12*
countries. Many Americans have both positive and negative ideas *13*
about their country. When they think of the lifestyle or the scenery *14*
(landscapes such as mountains or beaches at the ocean), they feel *15*
very positive and proud of their country. But sometimes, when they *16*
think about the government, they think about nuclear war and in- *17*
ternational problems. Then they have negative feelings about the *18*
country. *19*

  These images and ideas are all impressions of a country, the *20*
United States. People form these impressions in many different *21*

*Although technically more accurate, the term *North American* is not used by the people in the United States to describe themselves. Therefore, the term *American* is used throughout this book to describe things in the United States.

3 ways. They see American products and advertisements. They read 22
newspapers and hear people talk about the United States. They 23
probably see American movies and television shows. These impres- 24
sions are always changing. As people receive more information, they 25
adjust their images and concepts of a country. 26

4 Knowledge of a country includes many things. Typical prod- 27
ucts and actions by governments are part of this knowledge. But 28
the most important thing in learning about a country is knowledge 29
of the people of that country. What are their customs and lifestyles? 30
How do they raise their children? What are their values and beliefs? 31
How do they feel about work and entertainment, about time, about 32
friendships? 33

5 In this book you will read about many aspects of the United 34
States. You will read about lifestyles, institutions, values, and is- 35
sues which are all part of American life and culture. Before you be- 36
gin each chapter, think of your own impressions of the subject, 37
American women, American cities, American families. Use your own 38
impressions to compare with and question the impressions of the 39
authors. Contact the U.S.A. 40

The following vocabulary exercise will help you understand the meaning of new words in the reading without a dictionary.

D. Scanning/Vocabulary

DIRECTIONS: *It is important to be able to find information quickly when you read. This is scanning. Scan the reading for these words. Write the number of the line where you find them.*

Example: car ___4___ automobile _similar_____

Now look at the word on the right. Is its meaning similar or different from the meaning of car? The meanings of car and automobile are similar, so you write <u>similar</u> on the line. Remember that the word **similar** does not mean exactly the same; it means that the two words are close in meaning.

Try another example:

first ___1___ last _different_____

In this case, you find <u>first</u> in line 1 of the reading. The meanings are different, so you write **different** on the line. If you are not sure about the meaning of a word, read the sentence where you find it again. Try to understand its meaning from the other words in the sentence and the reading.

	LINE NUMBER		SIMILAR OR DIFFERENT?
1. thought	_____	idea	_____
2. image	_____	picture	_____
3. ideas	_____	concepts	_____
4. perhaps	_____	maybe	_____
5. positive	_____	negative	_____
6. scenery	_____	landscapes	_____
7. impressions	_____	first ideas	_____
8. form	_____	make	_____
9. includes	_____	has inside	_____
10. typical	_____	common	_____
11. products	_____	customs	_____
12. adjust	_____	change a little	_____
13. proud	_____	ashamed	_____
14. lifestyle	_____	institutions	_____
15. compare with	_____	look at side by side	_____

How much of the reading did you understand without using a dictionary? Do the next exercise to find out.

E. Reading Comprehension

DIRECTIONS: Circle the letter of the choice that best completes each sentence.

1. There are _____ examples given of images associated with the name *United States*.

    a. six   b. seven   c. eight

2. An example of a positive concept is _____.

    a. nuclear war   b. freedom   c. advertisement

3. According to the reading, Americans are _____ about their lifestyle.

    a. scenery   b. negative   c. happy

4. According to the author, Americans _____ have negative thoughts about their country.

   a. always   b. never   c. sometimes

5. The author thinks that you, the reader, have _____ the United States already.

   a. no knowledge of   b. many impressions of   c. negative ideas about

6. In paragraph 5, the author gives the idea that your ideas will _____.

   a. always be the same as the author's ideas   b. be wrong   c. sometimes be different from the author's ideas

7. People probably have _____ impressions of American involvement in other countries.

   a. positive   b. negative   c. no

8. Foreign business people probably think of an American _____ when they hear the words <u>United States</u>.

   a. product   b. landscape   c. institution

9. The term *American* is used because _____.

   a. North American is too long   b. people in the United States use it   c. the book is about Canada

10. People's impressions _____ when they learn more about a country.

   a. are negative   b. are never different   c. change

Look Again

Look at the corrected answers for the vocabulary exercise (exercise D) in section 1. Use the <u>similar</u> words to understand the meanings and to answer this vocabulary exercise. If the words in the following exercise are not in exercise D, look for them in the reading in order to understand their meanings. Do not use a dictionary.

A. Vocabulary

DIRECTIONS: Circle the letter of the choice that best completes each sentence.

1. I want to know more about the _____ of the people: what they do every day and how they spend their free time.

   a. work   b. lifestyle   c. products

2. My mother and my father work; _____ of my parents work.

   a. friendships   b. some   c. both

3. I am wearing a suit today because I want to make a good _____.

   a. involvement   b. custom   c. impression

4. Some people are happy about the changes, but _____ are unhappy.

   a. institutions   b. personals   c. others

5. On the train I looked out the window at the _____.

   a. scenery   b. products   c. customs

6. There are many different _____ to the problem. It is not easy to understand.

   a. images   b. aspects   c. people

7. Schools and churches are _____.

   a. lifestyles   b. institutions   c. landscapes

8. My parents are very _____ of me when I make good grades at school.

   a. positive   b. concept   c. proud

9. I am not _____ with him in any way.

　　a. involved　　　　　　b. entertained　　　　　　c. valued

10. The two men work in different fields of study. They are not _____ each other.

　　a. associated with　　　b. customs　　　　　　image of

React

Go back to the reading and put a question mark next to two or three sentences that you don't understand very well. Discuss these sentences with your classmates and teacher.

B. Vocabulary/Comprehension

DIRECTIONS: Complete the reading summary with words from this list. Try to complete it first without looking back at the reading.

aspects	ideas	knowledge
countries	image	lifestyles
freedom	impressions	negative
	institutions	product
		scenery

　　When people from other (1) _____ think about the United States, they probably have many different (2) _____. Some may have an (3) _____ of an American (4) _____ such as a big car or a hamburger. Others may think of American (5) _____ such as universities.

　　People in the United States are proud of the beautiful (6) _____. They are also proud of the political (7) _____ they have in this country, but some are concerned about American involvement in other countries.

　　The authors think that the most important thing in learning about another country is (8) _____ of the people in that

country: their customs and (9) _____. They want the
readers to think about their own ideas and (10) _____
when they read this book.

C. Think About It

DIRECTIONS: Answer the following questions.

1. In your opinion, what is important for you to learn about the United States?

2. Ask several people from other countries this question: "What is your first thought when you hear the name of my country, _____?"

3. Do people ever have <u>false</u> impressions about your country or the people in your country? <u>How</u> are their ideas wrong?

4. What are some things you are proud of when you think about your country?

D. Reading

DIRECTIONS: Read and answer the questions that follow.

An American company produced "instant" cake mixes, the kind of mix you add water to, bake 30 minutes, and have an "instant" cake. This product was very popular in the United States where homemakers liked fresh baked cakes but valued convenience and did not want to spend a lot of time cooking. The company decided to sell the cake mixes in the United Kingdom too. However, in the U.K., the "instant" cake mixes were not popular at all and the company lost money there with this product.

1. What do you think "instant" means?

2. Why do you think the cake mixes were unpopular in England?

3. Check the answers below. Now give your opinion—why did the company make this mistake?

Answers:
1. British homemakers have different values from American homemakers. They want to spend a lot of time cooking for their families so they did not want an "instant" cake product.
2. The company thought that Americans and British homemakers had the same values. People speak English in both countries, but the cultures of the U.S. and Britain are very different.

Contact a Point of View

A. Background Building

DIRECTIONS: Complete these sentences.

1. When I first came to the U.S., I was surprised because. . . .

2. I was <u>not</u> surprised to see. . . .

3. The thing which is most different for me in the U.S. is. . . .

Reading quickly is a very important skill. Remember to read groups of words—do not stop on individual words. You must read <u>and</u> complete the first exercise in five minutes, so you need to read <u>very</u> quickly. The statements in the exercise contain information connected to the reading.

11

This information is either *true* or *false* or it is *impossible to know* (because the reading does not give that information).

B. Timed Reading

DIRECTIONS: Read the following point of view and answer the questions in five minutes.

I am from Thailand. I am a student in an American university. This is my third year in the United States. After three years, it is difficult to remember my first impressions of the United States. But I noticed then and still notice now how much more informality there is in the United States than there is in Thailand.

Take, for example, clothes. I expected to see blue jeans because this is where they started, isn't it? But I didn't expect to see so many running shoes. People wear running shoes in classes, downtown, in expensive restaurants, and with business suits! I also couldn't believe the runners, joggers they call them, all over the place, but that gets into how Americans feel about health, which is another interesting concept.

If you think about the English language, you know that it is not a formal language. There is only one *you* and not a formal *you* for older people and an informal *you* for friends and children. I remember another thing that surprised me. My first English teacher in the United States was about fifty years old, but we called him *Al*, his first name. I wanted to call him Mr. Al, but he didn't like that. But not all situations are informal like this; in business and in certain professions like medicine things are more formal.

As a young person, I like the American idea of informality, but I think it will be better to be old in Thailand where people respect old people and have more formal relationships.

DIRECTIONS: Read each of the following statements carefully to determine whether each is true (T), false (F), or impossible to know (ITK).

1. _____ The writer is a woman.

2. _____ The writer is a university student.

3. _____ Al was the teacher's last name.

4. _____ The writer is young.

5. _____ The writer is married.

6. _____ The writer never saw running shoes downtown.
7. _____ The writer lived in the city of San Francisco.
8. _____ Americans call doctors by their first name.
9. _____ The writer has more ideas about Americans and health.
10. _____ The writer thinks formality is better for old people.

C. Vocabulary

DIRECTIONS: Circle the letter of the word(s) with the same meaning as the italicized word.

1. The way Americans feel about informality is an interesting *concept*.

   a. information   b. idea   c. aspect

2. I *noticed* a person sitting alone in the restaurant.

   a. saw   b. talked to   c. called

3. I know a lot of *runners*.

   a. bicycles   b. office people   c. joggers

4. They had a very old *friendship*.

   a. kind of relationship   b. understanding   c. belief

5. I have a good *impression* of her.

   a. general idea   b. custom   c. friendship

6. I never *start* my homework until 10:00 P.M.

   a. end   b. begin   c. try

7. Please give me *more* information.

   a. additional   b. good   c. better

8. I never *question* my father's ideas.

   a. answer   b. understand   c. ask about with doubt

9. This is an interesting *thought*.

   a. issue   b. quick idea   c. feeling

10. When my mother telephoned, I *immediately* told her the news.

    a. at the first moment   b. generally   c. slowly

D. React

DIRECTIONS: Answer these questions. Discuss them with a classmate.

1. What are some examples of informality?

2. Is your country formal or informal?

3. Do you think formality or informality is better? Why? In what situations?

E. Word Analysis

Part 1

DIRECTIONS: What shorter words can you see in these words?

Example: runner   _____ (run) _____

lifestyle	(1) ____ ____	freedom	(7) ____
informality	(2) ____	production	(8) ____
homemaker	(3) ____ ____	friendship	(9) ____
landscape	(4) ____	knowledge	(10) ____
newspaper	(5) ____ ____	action	(11) ____
comparison	(6) ____	advertisement	(12) ____

Part 2

DIRECTIONS: Read the following information about nouns and adjectives and then complete the exercise. Decide whether the italicized words are nouns or adjectives.

A **noun** is a word used to name something. For example, *girl, box, idea,* and *restaurant* are all nouns.

An **adjective** gives some information about a noun. For example, *good, interesting,* and *green* are all adjectives when they describe a noun.

	NOUN	ADJECTIVE
1. I live in a *small* apartment.	____	✓
2. *English* is difficult.	____	____
3. I am studying *English* history.	____	____
4. That is a *great* idea!	____	____
5. Many good things in life are *free*.	____	____

	NOUN	ADJECTIVE
6. I have a *negative* feeling about politics.	_____	_____
7. *Good* friends are life's greatest pleasure.	_____	_____
8. I never read the *newspaper* here.	_____	_____
9. Is that a typical *product* of your country?	_____	_____
10. My aunt is one of the *friendliest* people I know.	_____	_____

Look Back

A. Vocabulary

DIRECTIONS: Circle the letter of the choice that best completes each sentence.

1. I think that business is the best _____ to get into.

   a. lifestyle   b. profession   c. thought

2. My friend teaches in elementary school because she enjoys _____ with children.

   a. involvement   b. production   c. impressions

3. I am interested in this car because I saw the _____.

   a. impressions   b. advertisement   c. flags

4. It is difficult to talk about _____ in English.

   a. actions   b. concepts   c. institutions

5. I like the _____ in the mountains better than at the ocean.

   a. scenery   b. comparison   c. positive

6. What do you do for _____? Do you go to movies or stay at home?

   a. work   b. entertainment   c. association

7. I study at an English language _____.

   a. situation   b. institute   c. profession

8. When you travel long distances, it is difficult to _____ the time differences.

   a. notice   b. adjust to   c. involve

9. I don't have any _____ about the trip to New York.

   a. information   b. aspects   c. images

10. He did very strange things. His _____ frightened me.

    a. aspects   b. thoughts   c. actions

B. Matching

DIRECTIONS: Find the word or phrase in column B that has a similar meaning to a word in column A. Write the letter of that word or phrase next to the word in column A.

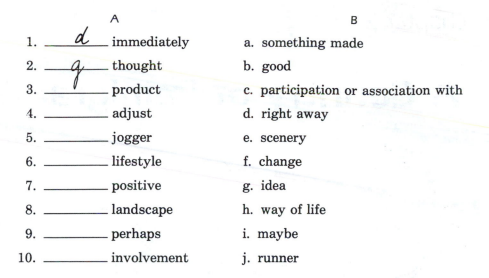

	A		B
1.	_d_ immediately	a.	something made
2.	_g_ thought	b.	good
3.	_____ product	c.	participation or association with
4.	_____ adjust	d.	right away
5.	_____ jogger	e.	scenery
6.	_____ lifestyle	f.	change
7.	_____ positive	g.	idea
8.	_____ landscape	h.	way of life
9.	_____ perhaps	i.	maybe
10.	_____ involvement	j.	runner

C. Synthesis Questions

1. What are some mistaken ideas people have about the customs in your country?

2. Do people in the United States ever do things that would be inappropriate in your country?

3. Write three questions that you have about the United States that you would like to answer.

4. Take a survey. Ask other people (classmates, teachers, people on the street) about their impressions of another country. For example, ask, "What is the first thing that you think of when you hear the names of these countries/cities: Rio de Janeiro; Thailand; etc. . . . "

D. Vocabulary Preview

DIRECTIONS: What shorter words can you see in these words from Chapter 2?

mixture	(1) _mix_	western	(6) _____
background	(2) _____ _____	neighborhood	(7) _____
downfall	(3) _____ _____	ownership	(8) _____
cowboys	(4) _____ _____	reservation	(9) _____
unwilling	(5) _____	racial	(10) _____

A Country of Immigrants

A First Look

A. Background Building

1. Ask your classmates questions about the illustration on the preceding page.

2. If you put cheese, milk and butter into a pot and cook it, what happens to these ingredients? Is the mixture smooth or lumpy?

3. The title of this chapter is "A Country of Immigrants." What kinds of people came to the U.S.? Where were they from? Why did they come? Complete this chart. Compare your information with a classmate's information.

NAME OF PEOPLE	NAME OF COUNTRY	WHY THEY CAME
_____	_____	_____
_____	_____	_____
_____	_____	_____

B. Topic

DIRECTIONS: *Before you begin to read, look at these topics. There is one topic for each paragraph. Look quickly at the reading to find these topics. Do not read every word at this point. Write the number of the paragraph next to the topic of that paragraph.*

1. _____ examples of different types of neighborhoods
2. _____ the different faces of immigrants in the United States
3. _____ diversity in American society
4. _____ history of immigration in the United States

C. Reading

DIRECTIONS: Now read.

1

As you walk along the street in any American city, you see
many different faces. You see Oriental faces, black faces, and white
faces. These are the faces of the United States, a country of immigrants from all over the world. Immigrants are people who leave
one country to live permanently in another country.

2

The first immigrants came to North America in the 1600s from
northern European countries such as England and Holland. These
people generally had light skin and light hair. They came to live in
North America because they wanted religious freedom. In the 1700s
and early 1800s immigrants continued to move from Europe to the
United States. At this time there was one group of unwilling immigrants, black Africans. These people were tricked or forced to
come to the United States, where they worked on the large farms
in the south. The blacks had no freedom; they were slaves. In the
1800s many Chinese and Irish immigrants came to the United
States. They came because of economic or political problems in their
countries. The most recent immigrants to the United States, the
Indochinese, Cubans, and Central Americans also came because of
economic or political problems in their own countries. Except for
the blacks, most of these immigrants thought of the United States
as a land of opportunity, of a chance for freedom and new lives.

3

In the United States, these immigrants looked for assistance
from other immigrants who shared the same background, language,
and religion. Therefore, there are neighborhoods in each U.S. city
made up almost entirely of one homogeneous ethnic group. There
are all Italian, all Puerto Rican, or all Irish neighborhoods in many
East Coast cities and all Mexican neighborhoods in the Southwest.
In Dearborn, Michigan, there is a large group of Lebanese. There
are racial neighborhoods such as oriental Chinatown in San Francisco and black Harlem in New York. There are also neighborhoods
with a strong religious feeling such as a Jewish part of Brooklyn in
New York. And, of course, there are economic neighborhood divisions; in American cities very often poor people do not live in the
same neighborhoods as rich people.

4

This diversity of neighborhoods in the cities is a reflection of
the different groups in American society. American society is a mixture of racial, language, cultural, religious, and economic groups.
People sometimes call America a *melting pot* and compare its society to a soup with many different ingredients. The ingredients
(different races, cultures, religions, and economic groups) suppos-

1
2
3
4
5
6
7
8
9
10
11
12
13
14
15
16
17
18
19
20
21
22
23
24
25
26
27
28
29
30
31
32
33
34
35
36
37
38
39
40

edly mix together to make a smooth soup. But, in reality, there are   *41*
a few lumps left in the soup.   *42*

React

Is there some information in the reading you want to
know more about? Underline the sentence(s) where you
find this information. Talk to your classmates and teacher
about it.

D. Scanning/Vocabulary

*DIRECTIONS: Scan the reading for these words. Write the number of the line where you
find them. Then compare its meaning in the sentence to the meaning of the
word(s) on the right. Are the words similar or different? Write <u>similar</u> or <u>dif-
ferent</u> on the line.*

1. black	2	white	*different*
2. immigrants		tourists	
3. such as		for example	
4. generally		usually	
5. unwilling		willing	
6. slaves		free people	
7. recent		close to now	
8. except for		but	
9. opportunity		chance	
10. assistance		help	
11. shared		had together	
12. entirely		completely	
13. homogeneous		all the same	
14. poor		rich	
15. diversity		variety	
16. supposedly		in reality	

E. Reading Comprehension

DIRECTIONS: Circle the letter of the choice that best completes each sentence.

1. Two people of the same race share the same _____.

   a. language   b. religion   c. color

2. The first immigrants in the United States were _____.

   a. black   b. religious people   c. Indochinese

3. The black Africans in North America were _____ immigrants.

   a. happy   b. unwilling   c. recent

4. Harlem is an example of a _____ neighborhood.

   a. religious   b. language   c. racial

5. Immigrants moved _____ other immigrants from their countries.

   a. close to   b. far away from   c. without

6. The most recent immigrants came because of _____ problems.

   a. racial   b. religious   c. political

7. There _____ rich and poor people in the same neighborhoods in the United States.

   a. are often   b. are not usually   c. are never

8. The topic of the third paragraph is _____.

   a. immigration   b. American society   c. neighborhoods in American cities

9. There were more _____ immigrants in the East.

   a. Irish   b. Chinese   c. Mexican

10. American society is _____.

    a. mixed   b. not completely mixed   c. not mixed at all

Look Again

A. Vocabulary

DIRECTIONS: Circle the letter of the choice that best completes each sentence.

1. Assistance is _____.

   a. religion   b. work   c. help

2. The East Coast and the Southwest are _____ of(in) the country.

   a. groups of people   b. parts   c. cities

3. An example of religion is _____.

   a. Jewish   b. black   c. Italian

4. A neighborhood is _____.

   a. an apartment building   b. a house   c. a city division

5. A society is _____.

   a. a group of people   b. immigrants   c. all American

6. An example of race is _____.

   a. Roman Catholic   b. white   c. Irish

7. A government problem is a _____ problem.

   a. political   b. street   c. forced

8. English is a _____.

   a. language   b. religion   c. literature

9. A minute is a _____ of an hour.

   a. mixture   b. group   c. division

10. A person with a lot of money is _____.

   a. economic   b. rich   c. poor

B. Reading Comprehension

DIRECTIONS: Complete this outline of the reading.

1. Introduction

   You see many different (1) _____ on the streets in the United

   States because it is a country of (2) _____.

2. Immigrants

   The first immigrants: from (3) _____.

   A group of unwilling immigrants: (4) _____.

   In the 1800s (5) _____ came because of (6) _____

   problems. The most recent immigrants, (7) _____, came be-

   cause of (8) _____ problems.

3. Neighborhoods

   In the East Coast, there are neighborhoods of all (9) _____. In

   the Southwest, there are all (10) _____ neighborhoods. In San

   Francisco and New York, (11) _____ and (12) _____

   are examples of neighborhoods made up of one race. An example of a religious

   neighborhood is in (13) _____ where most of the people are

   (14) _____.

4. Conclusion

   The writer thinks that American society is (15) mixed/not mixed.

C. Think About It

1. Do you know any immigrants or children of immigrants?

2. If yes, where do they live? Do they live near other people with the same background? The same language? The same religion?

3. Think of a neighborhood in a city in the United States and answer these questions.

   Name or location of the neighborhood: _____

   Is this neighborhood mixed or homogeneous? _____

   Type of people who live there: _____

4. What is the neighborhood like where you live?

D. Reading

DIRECTIONS: Look at Figure 1 and answer the questions below.

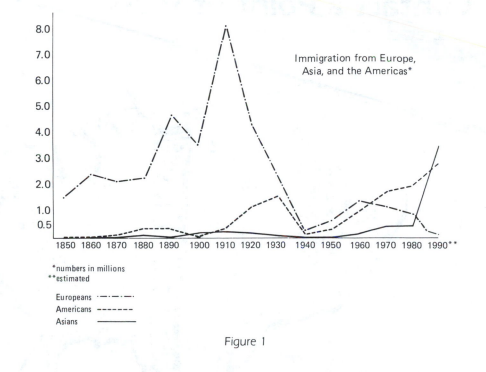

Figure 1

1. What information does Figure 1 show?

2. Which group, people from Europe, Asia, or the Americas, has had the most immigrants to the U.S.?

3. Between 1850 and 1860, about how many Europeans immigrated to the United States?

4. During what period was there the greatest amount of immigration?

5. At some time between 1841 and 1990, the American government passed a law limiting the number of immigrants who could come to the United States. By looking at the graph, can you guess when this happened? When?

6. During which period was European immigration lower than immigration (a) from the Americas? (b) from Asia?

7. According to Figure 1, which group has the most immigrants now?

Contact a Point of View

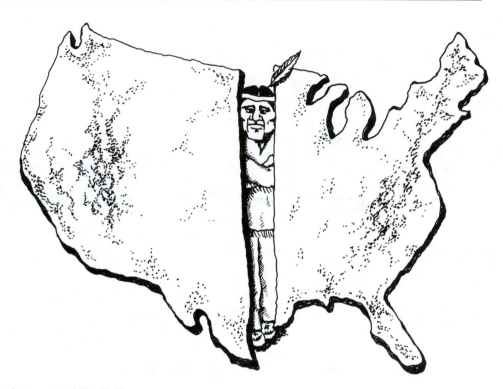

A. Background Building

1. The person in the above illustration is called a/an _____.

2. What do you know about the history of these people in the United States?

B. Timed Reading

DIRECTIONS: Read the following point of view and answer the questions in five minutes.

My name is Haske Noswood. I am a native American, a Navajo. You probably know native Americans as "Indians" and associate us with cowboys and western movies.

Most people forget that we were the first Americans, that we were here before any white men. Once, the Navajo and other native American groups lived well. Some of us hunted; some of us farmed. Most of us moved from place to place according to the season. We did not believe in land ownership. This was our downfall. We believed that land belonged to all people.

The white people thought differently. They came to our lands and divided it up among themselves. They took our land. We did not understand until it was too late. They tricked us and forced us all onto these reservations. They "gave" us this reservation land. There is reservation land all over the country. There is the Hopi reservation in Arizona and the Cherokee reservation in Tennessee. But this reservation land is almost always the worst land. They often put us on land that no one else wanted.

A lot of people have left the reservation to get good jobs or an education. But I am staying on the reservation because my people have many problems and I want to help them.

DIRECTIONS: Read each of the following statements carefully to determine whether each is true (T), false (F), or impossible to know (ITK).

1. _____ A reservation is a city.

2. _____ The Navajo reservation is in New Mexico.

3. _____ The Cherokee reservation is in Arizona.

4. _____ High taxes are one of the problems on the reservation.

5. _____ There are few opportunities for work on the reservation.

6. _____ Haske Noswood lives in New Mexico.

7. _____ All native Americans live in one area of the country.

8. _____ The reservation land is often bad land.

9. _____ Each native American owned a piece of land.

10. _____ Haske is a hunter.

C. Vocabulary

DIRECTIONS: Circle the letter of the word(s) with the same meaning as the italicized word(s).

1. What is the *real* problem?

   a. true   b. bad   c. difficult

2. I was *once* a farmer.

   a. never   b. always   c. at one time

3. This is *the worst* weather! It is really cold.

   a. very bad   b. very difficult   c. amazing

4. Spending money was my *downfall.*

   a. happiness   b. opportunity   c. biggest problem

5. He did *poorly* on his test.

   a. badly   b. well   c. hard

6. We will *divide* the house into apartments.

   a. sell   b. cut up   c. live

7. The farming *season* in the north is very short.

   a. place   b. time of year   c. area

8. I will *call* the baby John.

   a. number   b. tell   c. name

9. I *force* myself to study.

   a. push   b. continue   c. walk

10. I live *well* but I have little money.

   a. in a good way   b. poorly   c. hard

D. React

DIRECTIONS: Share your ideas with a classmate or with the class. Answer the following questions.

1. Who were the first people in your country?
2. How many different groups of people are there in your country now?
3. What is(are) the language(s) in your country?
4. What is(are) the race(s) in your country?
5. What is(are) the religion(s) in your country?

E. Word Analysis

Part 1

DIRECTIONS: Are the italicized words used as nouns or as adjectives?

	NOUN	ADJECTIVE
1. Salt is an *ingredient* used in cooking.	_____	_____
2. That is quite a *wealthy* neighborhood.	_____	_____
3. What is your *problem?*	_____	_____
4. He is a *native* of the United States.	_____	_____
5. My *native* language is English.	_____	_____
6. There is a large *group* of people outside.	_____	_____
7. What's the *difference?*	_____	_____
8. This is *your* book, isn't it?	_____	_____
9. What *color* is your hair?	_____	_____
10. My eyes are *brown*.	_____	_____

Part 2

1a. These prefixes change the meaning of a word from positive to negative:

Another example:

un-	willing	**un**willing	_____
in-	formal	**in**formal	_____
im-	possible	**im**possible	_____
dis-	agree	**dis**agree	_____

1b. Study the meanings of these:

| hetero- different | **hetero**geneous | _____ |
| homo- same | **homo**geneous | _____ |

The population in the United States is **heterogeneous**. In Japan, the population is more **homogeneous**.

2. Complete the sentences with one of the words from 1a or 1b.

   a. Our class is a(n) _____ group. We have students from many different countries.

b. Slaves were _____ immigrants to the United States.

c. Our ideas are completely different. I _____ with you.

d. I can't do that. I'm sorry, but it's _____ .

e. I have a(n) _____ lifestyle, so I don't have very many dressy clothes. I usually wear pants and a sweater.

f. In that new neighborhood, the people are all similar—they all have about the same income and are about the same age. They even drive the same kinds of cars. It's too _____ for me!

Look Back

A. Vocabulary

DIRECTIONS: Circle the letter of the choice that best completes each sentence.

1. Chicken and noodles are two _____ in chicken noodle soup.

   a. mixtures   b. divisions   c. ingredients

2. A group of people with many different religions, languages, and races is a _____ group.

   a. racial   b. cultural   c. mixed

3. He is a complete stranger to me. I don't know anything about his _____.

   a. concept   b. background   c. assistance

4. _____, the party will begin at 8:00 P.M., but I don't believe it.

   a. Typically   b. Supposedly   c. Positively

5. A class is a _____ of students.

   a. group   b. neighborhood   c. reflection

6. I want to buy the apartment building. Then I will be the _____.

   a. neighbor   b. assistant   c. owner

7. I came to this _____ because I wanted to live in a different area.

   a. place   b. mixture   c. division

8. He _____ lives here. He moved out of town last month.

   a. no longer   b. supposedly   c. permanently

9. She is a very _____ person. She goes to church twice a week.

   a. unwilling   b. political   c. religious

10. I like everything about my apartment _____ the cost. It is too expensive.

   a. with   b. except for   c. entirely

B. Matching

DIRECTIONS: *Find the word or phrase in column B which has a similar mean-ing to a word or phrase in column A. Write the letter of that word or phrase next to the word or phrase in column A.*

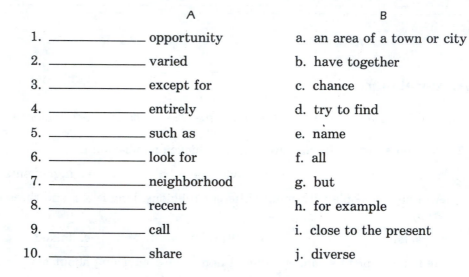

	A		B
1.	_____ opportunity	a.	an area of a town or city
2.	_____ varied	b.	have together
3.	_____ except for	c.	chance
4.	_____ entirely	d.	try to find
5.	_____ such as	e.	name
6.	_____ look for	f.	all
7.	_____ neighborhood	g.	but
8.	_____ recent	h.	for example
9.	_____ call	i.	close to the present
10.	_____ share	j.	diverse

C. Synthesis Questions

1. Interview other people (a classmate, your teacher, people on the street). Ask them about their background: where they were born; where their families were from; etc. . . . Work with your classmates to write in-terview questions.

2. Do you see examples of different kinds of people (religions, races, in-come level) living and working together in the United States or do you see examples of people staying apart because of these differences?

3. Find out more about native Americans. Go to the library or a museum and do research on this topic.

D. Vocabulary Preview

DIRECTIONS: *What shorter words can you see in these words from Chapter 3?*

employment (1) employ_____   unlike   (3) _____

movement   (2) _____   revitalize (4) _____

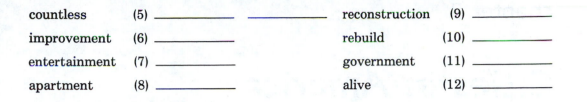

countless	(5) _____ _____	reconstruction	(9) _____
improvement	(6) _____	rebuild	(10) _____
entertainment	(7) _____	government	(11) _____
apartment	(8) _____	alive	(12) _____

chapter 3

Cities in America

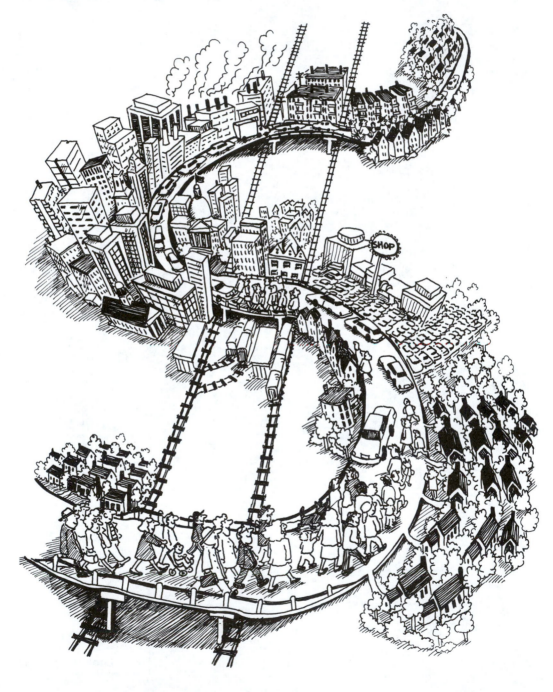

A First Look

A. Background Building

1. Where do you come from? From a city? From the suburbs (just outside the city) or from the country (far from a city)? _____

2. This chapter is about cities in America, but cities everywhere are similar. Write some impressions you have when you think about cities.

   _____

   _____

   _____

3. Which of your impressions are positive? Which are negative? Neutral?

B. Topic

DIRECTIONS: Before you begin to read, look at these topics. There is one topic for each paragraph. Look quickly at the reading to find these topics. Do not read every word at this point. Write the number of the paragraph next to the topic of that paragraph.

1. _____ population information
2. _____ cities are living again
3. _____ where people are moving now
4. _____ a description of cities
5. _____ a house in the suburbs
6. _____ a new type of city resident
7. _____ results of the move back to the cities

C. Reading

DIRECTIONS: Now read.

1

American cities are similar to other cities around the world: In every country, cities reflect the values of the culture. Cities contain the very best aspects of a society: opportunities for education, employment, and entertainment. They also contain the very worst parts of a society: violent crime, racial conflict, and poverty. American cities are changing, just as American society is changing.

2

After World War II, the population of most large American cities decreased; however, the population in many Sun Belt cities (those of the South and West) increased. Los Angeles and Houston are cities where population increased. These population shifts (the movement of people) to and from the city reflect the changing values of American society.

3

During this time, in the late 1940s and early 1950s, city residents became wealthier, more prosperous. They had more children so they needed more space. They moved out of their apartments in the city to buy their own homes. They bought houses in the suburbs (areas without many offices or factories near cities). During the 1950s the American "dream" was to have a house in the suburbs.

4

Now things are changing. The children of the people who left the cities in the 1950s are now adults. They, unlike their parents, want to live in the cities. Some continue to move to cities in the Sun Belt. Cities are expanding and the population is increasing in such states as Texas, Florida, and California. Others are moving to older, more established cities of the Northeast and Midwest, such as Boston, Baltimore and Chicago. The government, industry, and individuals are restoring old buildings, revitalizing poor neighborhoods, and rebuilding forgotten areas of these cities.

5

Many young professionals, doctors, lawyers, and executives, are moving back into the city. Many are single; others are married, but often without children. They prefer the city to the suburbs because their jobs are there; or they just enjoy the excitement and opportunities that the city offers. A new class is moving into the cities—a wealthier, more mobile class.

6

This population shift is bringing problems as well as benefits. Countless poor people must leave their apartments in the city because the owners want to sell the buildings or make condominiums, apartments which people buy instead of rent. In the 1950s, many poor people did not have enough money to move to the suburbs; now many of these same people do not have enough money to stay in the cities.

7

Only a few years ago, people thought that the older American cities were dying. Some city residents now see a bright, new future. Others see only problems and conflicts. One thing is sure: many dying cities are alive again.

1
2
3
4
5
6
7
8
9
10
11
12
13
14
15
16
17
18
19
20
21
22
23
24
25
26
27
28
29
30
31
32
33
34
35
36
37
38
39
40
41
42
43
44
45

React

In the reading choose one sentence that you find interesting and write it here. Talk about its meaning with a partner.

D. Scanning/Vocabulary

Part 1

DIRECTIONS: *Write the line number where you find the word(s). Then choose the best meaning for the word as it is used in that sentence.*

1. reflect   line number _____
   a. consider   b. shine   c. mirror

2. aspects   line number _____
   a. benefits   b. sides   c. concepts

3. opportunities   line number _____
   a. places   b. chances   c. needs

4. conflict   line number _____
   a. opposition   b. peace   c. issue

5. violent   line number _____
   a. using force   b. peaceful   c. difficult

6. space   line number _____
   a. yards   b. land   c. room

7. restoring   line number _____
   a. rebuilding   b. destroying   c. building stores in

8. countless   line number _____
   a. a few   b. many   c. homeless

9. shift   line number _____
   a. drive   b. change   c. action

10. alive   line number _____
    a. interesting   b. revitalized   c. dying

Part 2

DIRECTIONS: *Find a word that is the opposite of the one given. The line where you will find the word is given.*

1. line 4   best   _____
2. line 5   wealth   _____
3. line 8   increased   _____
4. line 14   poorer   _____
5. line 19   city   _____
6. line 21   similar to   _____
7. line 23   growing smaller _____
8. line 27   destroying   _____
9. line 32   boredom   _____
10. line 45   alive   _____

E. Reading Comprehension

DIRECTIONS: Circle the letter of the choice that best completes each sentence.

1. The author thinks that cities all over the world are _____.

   a. the same   b. similar   c. different

2. In paragraph 1, the author says that some good aspects of cities are schools, _____, and things to do.

   a. values   b. jobs   c. changes

3. The author gives _____ examples of the worst parts of a culture.

   a. two   b. three   c. four

4. The population of most large American cities _____ after World War II.

   a. decreased   b. increased   c. remained the same

5. The population in Houston and Los Angeles, _____ the population in most other cities, increased after the war.

   a. similar to   b. unlike   c. as well as

6. City residents became wealthier and more prosperous _____ World War II.

   a. during   b. after   c. before

7. In the 1950s many city residents wanted to _____.

   a. live in the suburbs   b. revitalize the city   c. live in apartments

8. Many people are now _____ the city.

   a. moving from   b. leaving   c. returning to

9. A few years ago, the cities were _____.

   a. alive   b. dying   c. entertaining

10. In paragraph 7, the author talks about the _____ of the city.

   a. bright future   b. benefits   c. opportunities

Look Again

A. Vocabulary

DIRECTIONS: Circle the letter of the choice that best completes each sentence.

1. The problem of divorce has many different _____.

   a. opportunities   b. benefits   c. aspects

2. The United States is a wealthy nation, but there is still _____ here.

   a. space   b. opportunity   c. poverty

3. I don't like living with a roommate. I'm moving _____ my family's house.

   a. back to   b. from   c. out of

4. She is _____ her sister; she is very tall and her sister is very short.

   a. similar to   b. unlike   c. like

5. One benefit of living in this apartment is that it has more _____.

   a. aspects   b. space   c. shifts

6. This box _____ many old books and souvenirs.

   a. reflects   b. explains   c. contains

7. The population of the world _____ daily.

   a. increases   b. inflates   c. decreases

8. Please don't _____ yet. It's still early.

   a. stay   b. leave   c. shift

9. Do you _____ your apartment or is it a condominium?

   a. shift   b. rent   c. buy

10. He has no job; he is looking for _____.

    a. excitement   b. employment   c. entertainment

B. Reading Comprehension

DIRECTIONS: *Mark these events in the order that they happened. Number 1 happened first, number 2 happened second, and so on through number 10.*

a. _____ They had large families.

b. _____ They moved to the suburbs.

c. _____ World War II ended.

d. _____ They wanted houses of their own.

e. _____ City residents became wealthier.

f. _____ Their children grew up.

g. _____ They wanted to live in the cities.

h. _____ They are rebuilding many cities.

i. _____ They are returning to the cities.

j. _____ They needed more space.

C. Think About It

1. Where do you find the following? In a city? The suburbs? The country? In all three?

   a. opportunities for good education _____

   b. condominiums _____

   c. quiet, open space _____

   d. factories _____

   e. a lot of crime _____

   f. racial conflict _____

   g. high cost of living _____

   h. opportunities for employment _____

   i. entertainment _____

   j. big houses _____

2. Where do you want to live in the future? In the city? In the suburbs? Or in the country?

3. What is important for you in this decision? Put number 1 next to the most important item, number 2 next to the second most important, and so forth.

_____ a lot of space   _____ convenience

_____ educational opportunities   _____ good apartments or houses

_____ entertainment and action   _____ beautiful scenery

_____ cost of living   _____ interesting people

_____ friendly neighbors   _____ (other) _____

_____ very little crime   _____

D. Graph Reading

DIRECTIONS: Look carefully at the chart of the population of seven cities in the United States (Figure 1). Answer the questions below.

City Population Chart: Seven U.S. Cities

	1970	1980	1984	Percent (%) change 80–84
Baltimore	905,000	787,000	764,000	−2.9
Boston	641,000	563,000	571,000	1.4
Chicago	3,369,000	3,005,000	2,992,000	.4
Houston	1,234,000	1,595,000	1,706,000	6.9
Los Angeles	2,812,000	2,967,000	3,097,000	4.3
Miami	335,000	347,000	373,000	7.4
Seattle	531,000	494,000	488,000	−1.1

Figure 1

1. Which city had the largest population in 1970? _____

2. Which city had the smallest population in 1970? _____

3. In which cities did the population increase in both 1980 and 1984?

_____

4. In which cities did the population decrease in both 1980 and 1984?

_____

5. In which cities did the population decrease in 1980 and increase in 1984?

_____

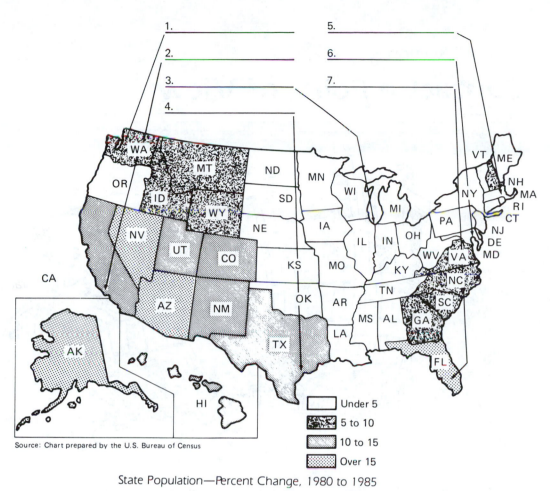

1. _____
2. _____
3. _____
4. _____
5. _____
6. _____
7. _____

	Under 5
	5 to 10
	10 to 15
	Over 15

Source: Chart prepared by the U.S. Bureau of Census

State Population—Percent Change, 1980 to 1985

Locate each of these seven cities on the map of the United States above and write its name on the line. The map shows the population change in the states where these cities are located. Write two facts that this map tells you.

1. _____

2. _____

How many of the states can you name where the population has increased more than 10 percent? Write them below.

_____   _____

_____   _____

_____   _____

_____   _____

Contact a Point of View

A. Background Building

DIRECTIONS: Look at the two buildings in the picture. Write as many words as you can to describe the two buildings.

CONDOMINIUMS FOR SALE	APARTMENTS FOR RENT
1.	1.
2.	2.
3.	3.
4.	4.

Where do most people live in major cities in your country? In houses? In apartments? Can you buy apartments? Apartments that you buy are called condominiums in the United States and they have become very popular recently.

B. Timed Reading

DIRECTIONS: Read the following point of view and answer the questions in four minutes.

Charlotte and Harry Johnson grew up in the city. They were neighbors as children, fell in love, and got married. They live in an apartment in their old neighborhood on the south side of town. They have two children, both boys. Harry is a bus driver and Charlotte is a waitress at a neighborhood restaurant.

Mr. Harley, their landlord, bought the apartment building back in the 1920s. The building is getting old now, and Mr. Harley wants to sell it and retire. A Mr. Chin wants to buy the building and make condominiums. He offered Mr. Harley $250,000 for the building. Mr. Harley wants to sell, but he's worried about the Johnsons. They're like family. He even knew their families before Harry and Charlotte were born. He knows they don't have the money and can't buy a condominium. He says, "The boys are like my own grandchildren. What can I do?"

Mr. Chin, of Chin Development Corporation, is a very important force in the revitalization of the south side of town. His company rebuilt the old factory area—a forgotten section of town. His work is bringing new residents and business to the south side. The Chin Development Corporation wants to buy the old apartment building from Mr. Harley. Mr. Chin is offering him a good price for the building. Of course, after reconstruction, the value of the building will increase greatly. "These people don't seem to want progress or improvements. We have to bring new, wealthier residents to the city to keep the city alive."

DIRECTIONS: Read each of the following statements carefully to determine whether each is true (T), false (F), or impossible to know (ITK).

1. _____ Charlotte and Harry lived in this neighborhood when they were children.

2. _____ They have two sons.

3. _____ Charlotte works in the neighborhood.

4. _____ Mr. Chin is offering two hundred and fifteen thousand dollars for the building.

5. _____ The Johnsons like Mr. Harley's family.

6. _____ Mr. Harley has no children.

7. _____ Mr. Chin wants to rent the apartments.

8. _____ He revitalized only the north side of the city.

9. _____ Mr. Harley bought the building in 1925.

10. _____ After reconstruction, the value of the building will decrease.

C. Vocabulary

DIRECTIONS: Circle the letter of the word(s) with the same meaning as the italicized word(s).

1. Mr. Harley is the *landlord*.

   a. renter   b. owner   c. custodian

2. The building is *getting* old.

   a. taking   b. shifting   c. becoming

3. He *is worried* about the Johnsons.

   a. doesn't care   b. is concerned   c. knows

4. They're *like* family.

   a. enjoyable   b. similar to   c. likable

5. Mr. Chin is a very important *force* in redevelopment.

   a. power   b. developer   c. buyer

6. His company rebuilt the old factory area—a *forgotten* section of town.

   a. revitalized   b. important   c. abandoned

7. The *value* of the building will increase after reconstruction.

   a. size   b. worth   c. shape

D. React

DIRECTIONS: Complete the following sentences based on the information in the timed reading.

There are two points of view in this reading.
1. Mr. Harley wants to. . . .
   Mr. Harley is worried because. . . .

2. Mr. Chin wants to. . . .
   Mr. Chin thinks that the old neighborhood and its residents. . . .

What is your point of view?
Mr. Harley should. . . .
Mr. Chin should. . . .
The Johnsons should. . . .

E. Word Analysis

Part 1

DIRECTIONS: Read the following information about verbs. Then decide if the italicized words in the sentences are nouns or verbs.

A **verb** expresses action (*walk, talk*) or relation (*be, seem*) involving other words. Every sentence has a verb.

	NOUN	VERB
1. Political attitudes often *shift* from left to right.	_____	_____
2. In the 1960s there was a sharp *increase* in crime.	_____	_____
3. What kind of *change* are you talking about?	_____	_____
4. The population *shift* to the Sun Belt occurred in the 1970s.	_____	_____
5. At that time population *increased* in the South, but decreased in the North.	_____	_____
6. *Progress* in this kind of weather is impossible.	_____	_____
7. Mobility means that people *move* from one situation to another.	_____	_____
8. The members reported little *progress* in the talks.	_____	_____
9. Don't make a *move!*	_____	_____
10. It sometimes seems that things *change* slowly.	_____	_____

Part 2

1. Study the meaning of these: Another example: _____

re-	again	rebuild	_____
		revitalize	
		reapply	
		review	
bene-	good	benefit	_____
		beneficial	

com-	together	community	_____
		committee	
con-		convention	
ven-	come	convention	_____
		invent	

2. Complete the sentences with one of the above words.

   a. We don't have classes today because all the teachers went to a _____
      _____.

   b. After the earthquake, they had to _____ the city.

   c. I have to _____ the vocabulary before the test.

   d. An additional _____ of living in the city is good schools.

   e. The president asked a _____ of seven people to study the
      problem and report back to him.

   f. Our neighborhood has a real sense of _____. We often have
      parties together and we cooperate on a lot of different projects.

   g. The university didn't accept me, but I'm going to _____
      next year.

Look Back

A. Vocabulary

DIRECTIONS: Circle the letter of the choice that best completes each sentence.

1. She is very kind to all the people who live on her street. She is very _____.

   a. neighborly   b. wealthy   c. reflective

2. I live near the city. I take the _____ bus and I get to the office in twenty minutes.

   a. revitalized   b. social   c. suburban

3. Yesterday I found an old table in my grandmother's house. It is old, but with some _____, it will be beautiful.

   a. employment   b. restoration   c. opportunity

4. We do not agree. We can't decide. Our ideas are _____.

   a. entertaining   b. conflicting   c. expanding

5. Condominiums are _____ for some city residents.

   a. mobile   b. rebuilding   c. beneficial

6. You must _____ productivity to earn money.

   a. decrease   b. contain   c. increase

7. He is a peaceful man. He doesn't like _____.

   a. entertainment   b. violence   c. opportunity

8. That movie is not good for children. It's a(n) _____ movie.

   a. modern   b. prosperous   c. adult

9. That apartment has many large rooms; it's very _____.

   a. residential   b. excitable   c. spacious

10. Poverty and _____ are negative aspects of modern city life.

    a. prosperity   b. violence   c. similarity

B. Matching

DIRECTIONS: Find the word or phrase in column B which has a similar mean- ing to a word or phrase in column A. Write the letter of that word or phrase next to the word or phrase in column A.

A	B
1. _____ reflect	a. prosperous
2. _____ wealthy	b. many
3. _____ area of residences	c. mirror
4. _____ people who live in a place	d. revitalize
5. _____ countless	e. part
6. _____ similar to	f. grow smaller
7. _____ decrease	g. population
8. _____ problem	h. have within
9. _____ rebuild	i. conflict
10. _____ number of people	j. residents
11. _____ aspect	k. neighborhood
12. _____ opportunities	l. like
13. _____ increase	m. grow larger
14. _____ benefit	n. advantage
15. _____ contain	o. chances

C. Synthesis Questions

1. Choose a city you would like to know more about. Go to the library and try to find information about this city in the encyclopedia or other books. Report to your classmates about the information you find.

2. Write a short letter to a city you would like to visit asking for infor- mation about that city. Try the city hall, the mayor's office, or the Chamber of Commerce. Where can you find addresses of cities in other states?

3. Plan a trip to a particular city by going to a travel agent to get bro- chures about that city. Where can you stay there? What can you see? Are there special sections of the city that are interesting? How can you get around that city? Are there famous places to see?

4. Look in the local newspaper to see what kind of housing there is in your area. Is it expensive to rent an apartment? Are there condominiums in your area? Houses? How do the prices compare with those in your home country?

5. Where do you think it is better to raise a family? In the city, in the suburbs, or in the country? Why?

D. Vocabulary Preview

What shorter words can you see in these words from Chapter 4?

popularity	(1) popular_____	international	(5) _____
addition	(2) _____	mixture	(6) _____
unhealthy	(3) _____	rediscovering	(7) _____
unchanging	(4) _____		

What words have a prefix that means not? (8) _____

Food in America

A First Look

A. Background Building

DIRECTIONS: *Wherever you come from, food is an important part of life. Think about your day yesterday and think about what you ate. Answer the following questions. Discuss them with your classmates.*

1. Did you eat breakfast? Yes   No   Alone?
   With family?   With friends?

2. If yes, what did you have? Drinks: coffee, tea, milk, juice
   Food: toast, cereal, eggs, pancakes, doughnuts

3. Did you eat lunch? Yes   No   Alone?
   With family?   With friends?

4. What did you have?

5. Did you eat dinner in a restaurant?   In a cafeteria?   At
   home?   Alone?   With family?   With friends?

6. What did you have?

7. If you ate at home, who cooked?

8. Ask your teacher what he or she had to eat yesterday. Does your
   teacher seem to like to eat healthy food or "junk" food?

B. Topic

DIRECTIONS: *Before you begin to read, look at these topics. There is one topic for each paragraph. Look quickly at the reading to find these topics. Do not read every word at this point. Write the number of the paragraph next to the topic of that paragraph.*

1. _____ fast food

2. _____ ethnic food

3. _____ traditional food in the United States

4. _____ a return to natural, unprocessed food

5. _____ changing attitudes about food

C. Reading

DIRECTIONS: Now read.

Many changes are taking place in "food styles" in the United
States. The United States is traditionally famous for its very solid
and unchanging diet of meat and potatoes. Now we have many different alternatives to choose from: various ethnic food, health food,
and fast food, in addition to the traditional home-cooked meal.

Ethnic restaurants and supermarkets are commonplace in the
United States. Because the United States is a country of immigrants, there is an immense variety. Any large American city is filled
with restaurants serving international cooking. Many cities even
have ethnic sections: Chinatown, Little Italy, or Germantown. With
this vast ethnic choice, we can enjoy food from all over the world.
This is a pleasant thought for those who come here to travel or to
work; they can usually find their native specialties: tabouli, arepas,
or miso soup. Besides sections of the cities, there are regions which
are well known for certain food because of the people who settled
there. For example, southern California has many Mexican restaurants, and Louisiana has a strong Creole accent to its food. (Creole
is a mixture of French, African, and Carribean Island food.)

Health food gained popularity when people began to think
more seriously about their physical well-being. The very term *health
food* is ironic because it implies that there is also "unhealthy" food.
Health food is fresh, natural, unprocessed food. It does not contain
preservatives to make it last longer or chemicals to make it taste
or look better. Most health food enthusiasts are vegetarians: They
eat no meat; they prefer to get their essential proteins from other
sources, such as beans, cheese, and eggs.

Fast-food restaurants are now expanding rapidly all over the
country. In the United States, speed is a very important factor. People usually have a short lunch break or they just do not want to
waste their time eating. Fast-food restaurants are places which take
care of hundreds of people in a short time. There is usually very
little waiting, and the food is always cheap. Some examples are
'burger and pizza places.

America's attitude toward food is changing, too. The traditional big breakfast and dinner at 6:00 P.M. are losing popularity.
People are rediscovering the social importance of food. Dinner with
family or friends is again becoming a very special way of enjoying

1
2
3
4
5
6
7
8
9
10
11
12
13
14
15
16
17
18
19
20
21
22
23
24
25
26
27
28
29
30
31
32
33
34
35
36
37

and sharing. Like so many people in other cultures, many Ameri-   38
cans are taking time to relax and enjoy the finer tastes at dinner,   39
even if they still rush through lunch at a hamburger stand.   40

React

Underline one idea which surprised you in the reading.
Tell the class why it surprised you.

D. Scanning/Vocabulary

Part 1

DIRECTIONS: Scan the reading for these words. Write the number of the line where you find the word. Then compare its meaning in the sentence to the meaning of the word(s) on the right. Are the words similar or different? Write similar or different on the line.

	LINE NUMBER		SIMILAR OR DIFFERENT
1. traditionally	_____	recently	_____
2. waste	_____	use with no benefit	_____
3. essential	_____	important	_____
4. unchanging	_____	fixed	_____
5. native	_____	foreign	_____
6. gained	_____	increased	_____
7. well-being	_____	health	_____
8. fresh	_____	processed	_____
9. vegetarian	_____	meat-eater	_____
10. taking time	_____	rush	_____

Part 2

DIRECTIONS: Find a word or words in the reading that has (or have) the same meaning as the word(s) below, and write it on the line. The number of the line is given to help you.

1. well-known (2)   _____
2. choices (4)   _____
3. different (4)   _____
4. usual (6)   _____
5. cultural (6)   _____
6. areas (10)   _____
7. enjoyable (12)   _____
8. strange (21)   _____
9. important (25)   _____
10. feeling (34)   _____

E. Comprehension

DIRECTIONS: Answer the following questions about each of the paragraphs in the reading.

Paragraph 1. Three categories of food are:

a. _____

b. _____

c. _____

Paragraph 2. In the United States, there is food from around the world. Give two examples:

a. _____

b. _____

Paragraph 3. Many people are now interested in health food. What is health food? _____

Paragraph 4. Fast food has become very popular.
Write two reasons why.

a. _____

b. _____

Paragraph 5. Americans are changing their feelings about food. Write two examples
how.

a. They _____

b. They _____

Look Again

A. Vocabulary

DIRECTIONS: Circle the letter of the choice that best completes each sentence.

1. She is always on television. She is a(n) _____ newscaster.

   a. traditional   b. essential   c. well-known

2. Fast-food restaurants are now _____.

   a. specialties   b. commonplace   c. factors

3. Immigration is an important factor in the _____ of ethnic restaurants.

   a. sharing   b. source   c. popularity

4. It is _____ that they call her *Smiley;* I never see her smile.

   a. ironic   b. alternative   c. various

5. It is _____ to have protein.

   a. traditional   b. ethnic   c. essential

6. Many people _____ energy; they use it without thinking.

   a. waste   b. rush   c. rediscover

7. *Fast food* _____ speed.

   a. contains   b. implies   c. takes care of

8. Don't buy that bread. It isn't _____.

   a. possible   b. fresh   c. processed

9. Meat is a _____ of protein.

   a. factor   b. taste   c. source

10. American Indians are _____ Americans.

    a. native   b. foreign   c. international

B. Reading Comprehension

DIRECTIONS: Circle the letter of the choice that best completes each sentence.

1. Meat and potatoes are examples of _____.

    a. the traditional
       American diet
    b. processed food
    c. health

2. Speed is a factor in the popularity of _____.

    a. our attitude
    b. lunch breaks
    c. fast-food restaurants

3. Germantown is an example of _____.

    a. international cooking
    b. an ethnic neighborhood
    c. a regional specialty

4. The author thinks that Americans are now eating dinner _____.

    a. at 6:00 p.m.
    b. more quickly
    c. later

5. Health food enthusiasts often _____.

    a. like meat
    b. are vegetarians
    c. eat processed food

6. People who come to the United States are pleased because _____.

    a. they can find
       their native food
    b. there are many
       regional specialties
    c. American food
       is traditional

7. Americans are relaxing at dinner, but they are still _____.

    a. rushing at lunch
    b. sharing it
    c. losing
       popularity

8. Two important factors in fast-food restaurants are _____.

    a. speed and cost
    b. expansions and
       lunch breaks
    c. 'burger and
       pizza places

9. _____ is a source of protein.

    a. Fruit
    b. Meat
    c. Natural food

10. An example of the traditional American attitude toward food is _____.

    a. a late lunch
    b. a quick lunch
    c. health food

C. Think About It

1. What are the most popular dishes in your country?

2. Is there fast food in your country? What is it like?

3. Which kind of food is eaten most often? Beef? Fish? Chicken?

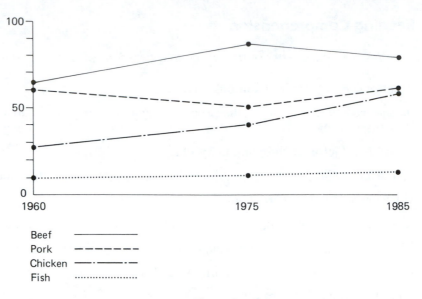

Beef ——————
Pork — — — — —
Chicken —·——·——·—
Fish ·················

Figure 1

D. Graph Reading

Part 1

What do Americans eat? Figure 1 from the U.S. Department of Agriculture can tell you.

DIRECTIONS: Read the graph in Figure 1 and answer the following questions.

1. Figure 1 shows changes in American eating style. What four foods are listed?

   _____   _____   _____   _____

2. According to the chart in Figure 1, which of the four is the most popular in the U.S.?

   _____

3. Which is the least popular? _____

4. Which of the four increased most in popularity? _____

5. Name one piece of information from Figure 1 that surprised you.

   _____

6. Would Figure 1 be different for people from your country? If not, why not? If yes, why? _____

Part 2

What do Americans drink?

DIRECTIONS: *Read the following information and then label the graph in Figure 2. Write the italicized words under the bar that each one refers to.*

In the year 1980, *soft drinks* such as colas were the most popular drinks in the United States consumed at the rate of 46 gallons per person per year. *Milk* was the next most popular drink at 27 gallons per person, followed by *coffee* at 25 gallons. *Tea* was at 6.8 gallons which is quite a bit below coffee. *Juice* was at 7.3 gallons. As for alcoholic drinks, *beer* was at 23 gallons per person. *Wine* was only slightly higher (2.5) than *other alcoholic drinks* (whiskey, vodka, etc.) which were the least popular of all drinks at 1.7 gallons per person.

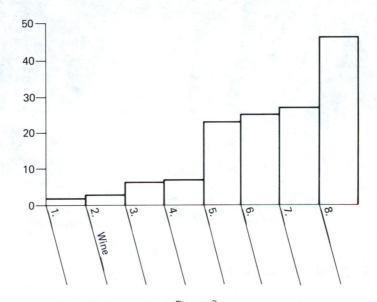

Figure 2

Contact a Point of View

A. Background Building

Popcorn, potato chips, and candy are favorite foods for lots of Americans. Food such as this, which does not have nutritional value for the body, is often called junk food—meaning worthless or without any value. Think about what you have eaten during the last 24 hours. Did you have any junk food?

B. Timed Reading

DIRECTIONS: Read the following point of view and answer the questions in four minutes.

All right! Enough cookies, cola, and chips! It seems that junk food is all that the children want to eat these days. Television controls their tastes. The kids see well-known personalities eating potato chips, candy, and other processed food, and they want to be like their heroes. How do they do it? They eat the same food. I wish there were more characters like old Popeye the sailor, who ate spinach and not french fries.

Just because I like brown rice, beans, and fresh vegetables, I don't expect my children to eat this "health food." I'm glad to cook traditional meals of meat and potatoes for them. I really can't be too upset with the kids because most adults aren't careful about what they eat. The other night, my wife and I went to a party where there was plenty to drink but very little for us to eat. They served hot dogs and hamburgers. I can't eat hot dogs, with all those preservatives, and hamburgers are filled with chemicals so that they look good. Besides the meat, they had sugar-filled cookies and cake, and, of course, chips. Terrible! I don't want the world to change because of me, but I think that people should realize that there are alternatives to eating meat. They always tell me that I probably don't get my essential proteins. But I feel better than ever and I'm sure that it's because I'm vegetarian. I would really like to see more television advertisements which show the benefits of good, healthy, natural food.

DIRECTIONS: Read each of the following statements carefully to determine whether each is true (T), false (F), or impossible to know (ITK).

1. _____ Cookies and chips are junk food.

2. _____ The author feels very healthy.

3. _____ Brown rice is junk food.

4. _____ Children want to eat junk food.

5. _____ The author eats meat.

6. _____ The author is married.

7. _____ Television influences children's food choice.

8. _____ Popeye ate only junk food.

9. _____ There are many TV advertisements for health food.

10. _____ If necessary, the author will serve meat and potatoes to the kids.

C. Vocabulary

DIRECTIONS: Fill in the blanks in the sentences with vocabulary from the reading. Make necessary changes in the form of the word.

1. processed/junk/taste/spinach

   _____ is not _____ food; it

   _____ good because it is not _____

   or treated with chemicals.

2. essential/careful/enough/plenty

   People should be _____ about getting _____

   _____ of _____ proteins. Many people do not get

   _____.

3. fresh/expect/upset

   She was _____ at the restaurant because she

   _____ to get _____ vegetables,

   not canned ones.

4. personalities/heroes/influence

   Many children's _____ are TV _____.

   These people often _____ the attitudes of the children.

D. React

> *DIRECTIONS: America's attitude toward food is different from many other countries. Have you changed your "food style" in the United States? Put a check beside the following statements that are true for you. Share your ideas with a classmate or with the class.*

In the United States, I eat

_____ more	_____ less
_____ more meat	_____ less meat
_____ more junk food	_____ less fresh food
_____ more frozen food	_____ fewer sweets
_____ more canned food	
_____ more at breakfast	_____ less at breakfast
_____ more at lunch	_____ less at lunch
_____ more at dinner	_____ less at dinner
_____ a faster breakfast	_____ a later breakfast

_____ an earlier lunch in
            restaurants

_____ a later dinner

_____ more often

_____ less often

In the United States, I ate some things for the first time.

I really like _____.

I really hate _____.

E. Word Analysis

Part 1

DIRECTIONS: *Look at the endings for* **adjectives** *below. Are the italicized words in the sentences adjectives or nouns?*

NOUNS	ADJECTIVES
success	success*ful* (full of)
value	value*less* (without)
religion	religi*ous*

Note that -*ful* and -*less* cannot be added to all nouns. For example, "valueful" is not a word, but valueless is.

	NOUN	ADJECTIVE
1. His work is always *careless* and messy.	_____	_____
2. That's a *wonderful* idea.	_____	_____
3. A *thoughtful* person is one who is kind.	_____	_____
4. There are *various* possibilities for the party.	_____	_____
5. Everyone was shocked. It was a *senseless* murder.	_____	_____
6. He does everything with *care*.	_____	_____
7. How important is *success?*	_____	_____
8. Only a few things in life are *changeless*.	_____	_____
9. That diamond is a *priceless* antique.	_____	_____
10. She watched the kitten with *wonder*.	_____	_____

Part 2

DIRECTIONS: *In other chapters, you have studied parts of the* **boldfaced** *words in the sentences. Write the letter of the meaning of the word from the list following the sentences.*

1. Street noise is one of the **disadvantages** of living in the city. _h_

2. Many people have gone to a university on the scholarships your company established, so the **benevolence** of your company is well-known. _____

3. The milk in this country is **homogenized.** Cream is sold in a separate bottle. _____

4. Some universities in the United States have **coeducational** dormitories. _____

5. Studies show that smoking cigarettes is **unhealthy.** _____

6. The union disagreed with parts of the contract, so the union and the company will have to **renegotiate** the contract. _____

7. All the scientists **convened** at a meeting in Geneva. _____

8. The **community** _____ is quite **heterogeneous** _____ so my children are learning to accept different customs and values.

9. The children **dislike** _____ each other, but they usually **cooperate** _____ with me.

a. negotiate again
b. came together
c. group of people living in the same area
d. do not like
e. wish to do good
f. different from each other

g. mixed well
h. bad things, not an advantage
i. not healthy
j. work together well
k. male and female students together

Look Back

A. Vocabulary

DIRECTIONS: Circle the letter of the choice that best completes each sentence.

1. He is a strong, _____ candidate for the presidency.

   a. commonplace   b. solid   c. rushed

2. Using a lot of electricity is _____.

   a. rediscovering   b. wasteful   c. well known

3. The Pacific Ocean is very _____.

   a. processed   b. expansive   c. gaining

4. The food is inexpensive but _____.

   a. tasty   b. social   c. structured

5. He dislikes everything; he has a very poor _____.

   a. well-being   b. popularity   c. attitude

6. There are _____ immigrant groups in most large American cities.

   a. various   b. unchanging   c. popular

7. What kind of _____ does that pie have?

   a. filling   b. importance   c. pleasantness

8. _____ is important in fish.

   a. Control   b. Freshness   c. Diet

9. _____ is an important factor for most movie personalities.

   a. Fame   b. Gain   c. Irony

10. The _____ of life is a question for all human beings. What is life's meaning?

   a. waste   b. essence   c. attitude

B. Matching

DIRECTIONS: *Find the word in column B which has a similar meaning to a word in column A. Write the letter of that word next to the word in column A.*

	A		B
1. _____ upset		a. important
2. _____ essential		b. use poorly
3. _____ ironic		c. rush
4. _____ minimal		d. worried
5. _____ immense		e. large
6. _____ waste		f. strange
7. _____ alternative		g. well known
8. _____ famous		h. grow
9. _____ hurry		i. plenty
10. _____ expand		j. commonplace
11. _____ usual		k. choice
12. _____ a lot		l. almost none

C. Synthesis Questions

1. What kind of food do you miss most from home? If you could have any dish from home right now, what would it be?

2. Many people say that they really like ice cream in the United States. Do you have a favorite American dish?

D. Vocabulary Preview

DIRECTIONS: What shorter words can you see in these words from Chapter 5?

specialist	(1) _____	friendliness	(5) _____
unlucky	(2) _____	intercultural	(6) _____
unfamiliar	(3) _____	knowledge	(7) _____
newcomers	(4) _____	unreality	(8) _____

familiarity	(9) _____	disorientated	(12) _____
successful	(10) _____	homesick	(13) _____
impression	(11) _____	illness	(14) _____

(15) international, intercultural: inter means _____

　　　Another example: _____

(16) self-conscious, self-image: self means _____

　　　Another example: _____

E. Skimming

Look quickly at the next page. Answer these questions.

1. What is this page?
2. How is it organized?

F. Scanning

Answer these questions as quickly as possible.

1. How many different kinds of restaurants are listed here?
2. What is the name of an Indonesian restaurant?
3. Which restaurants recommend reservations?
4. Where is Zola located?
5. How many Japanese restaurants are there?
6. Which restaurants are open after midnight?
7. Which restaurant serves Kirin beer?
8. How many health food restaurants are listed?
9. Is Assad's an Indian restaurant?
10. Where would you like to eat tonight?

RESTAURANTS
A guide arranged by cuisine

Chinese

BEIJING 200 Center St............................225-5877
DRAGON INN 15 Pleasant.......................259-1134
POLYNESIAN VILLAGE
  Chinese and Polynesian Cuisine
  Luncheon Specials
  209 Sidney Ave.......................................567-6892
WOK AWAY 54 Spring............................223-9987

Fast Food

BURGER AND COKE
  15 Roosevelt Ave.....................................277-7896
SAL'S SUBS
  Best Subs in Town!
  2326 Michigan Dr 287-8777
PIZZA PARLOR
  Open Until 3:00 AM
  654 Doolittle St.......................................261-4837

French

AUTRE MOMENT
  Recommended by CITY MAGAZINE
  Function Room Private Parties
  1 Bedford Place......................................553-1674
BRASSERIE FRANCAIS 13 Dresser St......233-1667
CHEZ FRANCINE
  Elegant Dining Thurs - Sat.
  Reservations Recommended
  28 Simon St...245-1562
LE SANDWICH 2 Cook St..........................264-9981
ZOLA 5 Pinyon Place................................245-1943

German

HAUFBRAU 1779 Dwight Ave.................256-1329

Greek

ACROPOLIS
  Lunch and Dinner
  11:00 AM to Midnight
  A Taste of the Greek Islands
  653 Fourth Ave.......................................295-5968

Health Food

ALICE'S KITCHEN
  Near Uptown Shopping Center
  23 Arlington..299-1563

NATURAL NUTRITION 1225 East 3rd.....215-1967
WHOLE EARTH EATERY
  All Natural Ingredients
  Open for Lunch and Dinner
  9 Knox St...223-1647

Indian

CURRY PALACE
  1276 Fourth St. Old Town.......................345-6719
TAJ MAHAL
  India at Its Best
  3390 New London St................................557-8030
TASTE OF INDIA 4 Madison Park............467-1378
ROYAL INDIA
  Open Until 1:30 AM
  7890 Hirsch...498-1984

Indonesian

JAKARTA RESTAURANT Park Ave........345-6767

Japanese

KYOTO RESTAURANT
  Shushi/Sashimi/Kirin Beer
  3447 Elliot Ave..234-1456
SAMURAI 14 New Britton St.................879-1457
GEISHA INN
  Call For Reservations
  13 Squire Rd...897-3546
MIKA 5659 Cutler Ave..............................786-1543
TEMPURA 4897 King SW.........................239-8767
HANA RESTAURANT 11402 18th St.......342-1223

Mexican

CASA LOPEZ
  433 Drummer Blvd. Sea Town.................677-5645
THE CHILE FACTORY
  Best Salsa in Town
  850 Marion Way 245-6778
PACO'S 18 Dwight....................................459-4545
TORTILLA EXPRESS
  Johnson Ave at Millbrook........................345-5867

Middle East

FALAFAL 455 Bruce Dr............................455-6778
ASSAD'S 19987 Spring Valley Parkway.....564-3467
SAID'S SANDWICHES 1675 Murdock St...456-4545

chapter 5

Culture Shock

A First Look

A. Background Building

DIRECTIONS: *Answer these questions about yourself. The ones on this page are about your first days in the U.S. The ones on the next page are about how you feel now.*

My first days in the U.S.

I _____ life in America.

    a. loved   b. hated   c. had no strong feelings about

I _____ being with Americans.

    a. loved   b. hated   c. had no strong feelings about

I _____ English.

    a. loved   b. hated   c. had no strong feelings about

I _____ homesick most of the time.

    a. was not   b. was

I wanted to spend my time with _____.

    a. Americans   b. people from my culture

I wanted to speak _____.

    a. English   b. my language

I thought life in America was _____.

    a. wonderful   b. terrible

I thought Americans were _____.

    a. wonderful   b. terrible

I _____ to go home after one week.

    a. didn't want   b. wanted

Count your "a" answers and your "b" answers. a. _____ b. _____

NOW

I _____ life in America.

    a. love   b. hate   c. have no strong
                                                                   feelings about

I _____ being with Americans.

    a. love   b. hate   c. have no strong
                                                                   feelings about

I _____ English.

    a. love   b. hate   c. have no strong
                                                                   feelings about

I _____ homesick most of the time.

    a. am not   b. am

I want to spend my time with _____.

    a. Americans   b. people from my culture

I want to speak _____.

    a. English   b. my language

I think life in America is _____.

    a. wonderful   b. terrible

I think Americans are _____.

    a. wonderful   b. terrible

I _____ to go home in one week.

    a. don't want   b. want

Count your "a" answers and your "b" answers. a. _____   b. _____
The title of this chapter is "Culture Shock." What do you think that means?

B. Topic

DIRECTIONS: Before you begin to read, look at these topics. There is one topic
for each paragraph. Look quickly at the reading to find these
topics. Do not read every word at this point. Write the number
of the paragraph next to the topic of that paragraph.

    1. _____ the people who experience culture shock

    2. _____ the things people say when you leave home

3. _____ three stages of culture shock

4. _____ the feelings of culture shock

5. _____ problems in a new culture

6. _____ definition of culture shock

C. Reading

DIRECTIONS: Now read.

1   "You're going to the United States to live? How wonderful! You're really lucky!"

    Does this sound familiar? Perhaps your family and friends said similar things to you when you left home. But does it seem true all the time? Is your life in this new country always wonderful and

2 exciting? Specialists in counseling and intercultural studies say that it is not easy to adjust to life in a new culture. They call the feelings which people experience when they come to a new environment *culture shock.*

    According to these specialists, there are three stages of culture shock. In the first stage, the newcomers like their environment.

3 Then, when the newness wears off, they begin to hate the city, the country, the people, the apartment, and everything else in the new culture. In the final stage of culture shock, the newcomers begin to adjust to their surroundings and, as a result, enjoy their life more.

    Some of the factors in culture shock are obvious. Maybe the weather is unpleasant. Perhaps the customs are different. Perhaps the public service systems such as the telephone, post office, or transportation are difficult to figure out and you make mistakes. The simplest things seem difficult. The language may be difficult. How many times have you just repeated the same thing again and again and hoped to understand the answer eventually? The food may seem strange to you and you may miss the familiar smells of the food you are accustomed to in your own country. If you don't

4 look similar to the natives, you may feel strange. You may feel like everyone is watching you. In fact, you are always watching yourself. You are self-conscious.

    Who experiences culture shock? Everyone does in some form or another. But culture shock comes as a surprise to most people. A lot of the time, the people with the worst culture shock are the people who never had any difficulties in their own countries. They

5 were active and successful in their community. They had hobbies or pastimes which they enjoyed. When they come to a new country, they do not have the same established positions or hobbies. They

find themselves without a role, almost without an identity. They *35*
have to build a new self-image. *36*

6

Culture shock produces a feeling of disorientation. This dis- *37*
orientation may be homesickness, imagined illness, or even para- *38*
noia (unreasonable fear). When people feel the disorientation of cul- *39*
ture shock, they sometimes feel like staying inside all the time. They *40*
want to protect themselves from the unfamiliar environment. They *41*
want to create an escape within their room or apartment to give *42*
themselves a sense of security. This escape does solve the problem *43*
of culture shock for the short term, but it does nothing to familiar- *44*
ize the person more with the culture. Familiarity and experience are *45*
the long-term solutions to the problem of culture shock. *46*

React

1. Look at the reading. Underline a sentence you agree with.
2. Underline a sentence you don't understand.
3. Discuss these sentences with your classmates and teacher.

D. Scanning/Vocabulary

PART 1

DIRECTIONS: *Write the line number where you find the word(s). Then choose the best meaning for the word as it is used in that sentence.*

1. specialists   line number _____

   a. authorities   b. important people   c. doctors

2. environment   line number _____

   a. place around   b. time you live in   c. country
   you

3. stages   line number _____

   a. part of a theater   b. progressive parts   c. transportation

4. final   line number _____

   a. most important   b. most difficult   c. last

5. obvious   line number _____

    a. easy to see   b. difficult   c. factors

6. figure out   line number _____

    a. see   b. design   c. understand

7. self-conscious   line number _____

    a. aware of   b. embarrassed   c. homesick
      yourself

8. role   line number _____

    a. part in a play   b. friend   c. position

9. paranoia   line number _____

    a. good feeling   b. imagined illness   c. unreasonable fear

10. term   line number _____

    a. condition   b. word or expression   c. length of time

Part 2

DIRECTIONS: Find a word that is the opposite of the one given. The line where you will find the word is given.

1. line 2   unlucky   _____

2. line 11   native   _____

3. line 20   most difficult   _____

4. line 23   forget   _____

5. line 30   best   _____

6. line 32   lazy   _____

7. line 38   real   _____

8. line 42   destroy   _____

E. Reading Comprehension

DIRECTIONS: Circle the letter of the choice that best completes each sentence.

1. There are apparently _____ stages of culture shock.

    a. two   b. three   c. four

2. People who come to a new environment _____ feel lucky and happy.

    a. do not always   b. always   c. never

3. According to the author, it _____ easy to adjust to a new culture.

   a. is always   b. is usually   c. is not

4. The author gives _____ examples of public service systems.

   a. two   b. three   c. four

5. Someone who looks _____ the natives of a country may feel strange.

   a. similar to   b. at   c. different from

6. People in a foreign culture feel _____ about themselves and their positions.

   a. differently   b. the same   c. happy

7. The author gives _____ examples of the disorientation of culture shock.

   a. two   b. three   c. four

8. The author thinks that it is _____ idea for people feeling culture shock to stay in their homes as a long-term solution to culture shock.

   a. not a good   b. a great   c. not a bad

9. In the final stage of culture shock, people _____ the new environment.

   a. love   b. adjust to   c. hate

10. People who feel culture shock stay at home because of _____.

   a. insecurity   b. solutions   c. the weather

Look Again

A. Vocabulary

DIRECTIONS: Circle the letter of the choice that best completes each sentence.

1. In this reading, a specialist is probably _____.

   a. a doctor   b. an authority   c. a newcomer

2. Your _____ is the area around you.

   a. environment   b. culture   c. self-image

3. Disorientation is a feeling of _____.

   a. security   b. knowledge   c. unreality

4. I can't figure out my homework. I can't _____ it.

   a. remember   b. escape from   c. understand

5. I am bored. My life is not _____ enough.

   a. experienced   b. active   c. essential

6. People usually have hobbies for _____.

   a. money   b. enjoyment   c. a job

7. A newcomer is _____ with the area around him or her.

   a. unfamiliar   b. unhappy   c. accustomed to

8. When you feel that everyone is watching you, you are _____.

   a. secure   b. self-conscious   c. unfamiliar

9. Paranoia is a feeling of _____.

   a. fear   b. happiness   c. experience

10. I don't know him. I don't know his _____.

    a. system   b. identity   c. term

B. Reading Comprehension

DIRECTIONS: Complete the reading summary with words from this list. Try to complete it first without looking back at the reading.

adjusting	hating	shock
different	liking	short-term
experience	long-term	solution
familiarity	problems	sometimes

(1) _____ to a new culture is not easy. The (2) _____ of adjusting to a new environment is called culture (3) _____. There are three stages of culture shock: (4) _____ the new environment, (5) _____ it, and adjusting to it. People experience culture shock because of (6) _____ customs, weather and food, and language (7) _____. (8) _____ the people with the worst culture shock are people who never had any difficulties in their own country. The (9) _____ (10) _____ to culture shock is to stay at home and try to escape. The (11) _____ solutions are (12) _____ and experience.

C. Think About It

DIRECTIONS: Discuss the answers to these questions with your classmates.

1. What was your favorite hobby or pastime when you were in your country? Is it possible to do that in the United States?

2. Is there any activity that you enjoy (or might enjoy) doing in your free time in the United States? What is that? How difficult or expensive is it to do?

3. How much time do you spend in your room, house, or apartment?

D. Reading

DIRECTIONS: Read and answer the questions below.

Jody and her family spent a year in England while her husband was in a graduate program there. They lived in a friendly community and traveled to a lot of interesting places in the U.K. and in Europe. Back at home in the United States, Jody told her friends about their wonderful year. She said that England was a great place to spend a year, even though she wouldn't want to live there permanently. Jody was happy to be home, but she felt strange. Even one month after her trip, she didn't have any energy and kept doing stupid things—she left her wallet at stores twice and forgot to meet people for lunch and other appointments. She didn't feel like cooking and she spent a lot of time sleeping.

1. Where is Jody's home?

2. Did she have a good time in her year in England? Why or why not?

3. What do you think was the problem for Jody when she came back home? (answer below)

4. What can Jody do to feel better? (answer below)

Answer to 3: Jody was suffering from the *fourth* stage of culture shock—the readjustment people have when they return to their countries.

Answer to 4: Jody will feel better after a while. She needs time to put her trip into perspective and adjust to her normal life in the United States.

Contact a Point of View

A. Background Building

1. What do you think the above illustration means?

2. Do you ever feel like the person in the illustration? Why or why not?

B. Timed Reading

DIRECTIONS: *Read the following point of view and answer the questions in four minutes.*

Nguyen Chau Van Loc came to the United States in 1979 from Vietnam. His first impression of the United States was very positive. He was particularly impressed with the way Americans had put technology to work for them. Americans made machines to take them upstairs and downstairs, give them money at the bank, and even open doors for them. He felt that this new environment offered him many exciting opportunities.

However, Loc quickly found himself unprepared to take advantage of these opportunities. He knew almost no English. Even when he knew what to say on a bus or in a store, no one understood him and he had to repeat and repeat. In Vietnam, Loc was a technician, but in the United States he did not have enough experience compared with other people. He had trouble finding a job. He felt that he did not have an important role or position in the city and missed the security and friendliness of his town in Vietnam. He felt that he would never learn English or feel happy in the United States. He began to feel very depressed and homesick.

Loc was lucky because there was a counselor in his English program. This counselor helped Loc to understand that his feelings were normal and that they were only a stage in his adjustment to this new culture. Loc began to look around him and to talk to other Vietnamese. He saw that many others felt the same way he did. Some, in fact, were more disoriented than he was and were afraid to go out into the city.

Eventually, Loc began to feel better about his life in the United States. He developed a position in the Vietnamese American community and adjusted to his new role in American society. He is accustomed to his life in this new country but will always miss Vietnam.

DIRECTIONS: Read each of the following statements carefully to determine whether each is true (T), false (F), or impossible to know (ITK).

1. _____ Loc came from Vietnam.

2. _____ Loc is married.

3. _____ Loc came to the United States in 1977.

4. _____ Loc had a positive attitude about American technology.

5. _____ Loc did not have a job in Vietnam.

6. _____ A counselor helped Loc.

7. _____ The counselor was a woman.

8. _____ No one felt the same way that Loc did.

9. _____ People understood Loc's English easily.

10. _____ Loc never thinks about Vietnam now.

C. Vocabulary

DIRECTIONS: Circle the letter of the word(s) with the same meaning as the italicized word(s).

1. My first *impression* of the teacher was good.

   a. experience with   b. conversation with   c. ideas about

2. American *technology* surprised the Vietnamese immigrant.

   a. scientific development   b. machines   c. industry

3. There are many *opportunities* for work in the city.

   a. possibilities   b. difficulties   c. advantages

4. I wrote my homework *again*.

   a. very well   b. another time   c. finally

5. He felt *self-conscious* when he spoke English.

   a. strong   b. tired   c. insecure

6. He was not sure of his *role* in the group.

   a. position   b. friend   c. pay

7. I am always *depressed* on rainy days.

   a. angry   b. tired   c. sad

8. The *counselor* talked to me about my problems.

   a. assistant   b. advisor   c. teacher

9. The newcomers felt *disoriented* in the airport.

   a. mixed up   b. happy   c. homesick

10. The *image* on this television is bad.

   a. picture   b. actor   c. color

D. React

DIRECTIONS: When you entered a new environment or culture, what was the most difficult thing you experienced? What was the easiest? Number these things according to the level of difficulty. Write 1 for the hardest and 10 for the easiest. Include all the numbers from 1 to 10.

_____ the bank

_____ the transportation system

_____ the post office

_____ the living situation (roommates, finding a place to live, neighbors)

_____ making friends

_____ the weather

_____ understanding American customs and lifestyles

_____ understanding American values and beliefs

_____ using the telephone

_____ finding good food to eat

Explain to the other people in your class why you had difficulties with your number 1, the hardest thing. Give examples of your experiences. After you were in this new environment for a while or even now, what was or is the most difficult thing for you? Did the most difficult thing become easier in time or did it stay the same?

E. Word Analysis

Part 1

DIRECTIONS: *Look at the endings for nouns and adjectives below. Are the italicized words in the sentences nouns or adjectives? Remember that there is never an s̲ on the ends of adjectives in English.*

NOUN	ADJECTIVE
soci*ety*	soci*al*
tradi*tion*	traditional

	NOUN	ADJECTIVE
1. This solution will be *beneficial* for everyone.	_____	_____
2. Our sense of *community* is very important.	_____	_____
3. *Poverty* is a serious social problem.	_____	_____
4. *Racial* conflict is an issue in the United States.	_____	_____
5. She is always very *practical.*	_____	_____
6. Downtown is the *central* business area.	_____	_____

	NOUN	ADJECTIVE
7. What is a *typical* name in your country?	_____	_____
8. There is some *similarity* between you and your brother.	_____	_____
9. Who has *control* here?	_____	_____
10. People in certain countries value *formality* greatly.	_____	_____

Part 2

1. Study the meanings of these:

Another example:

inter-	between	**inter**cultural **inter**personal	_____
tele-	distance	**tele**vision **tele**scope	_____
vid- vis-	to see	tele**vis**ion e**vid**ent	_____
phon-	sound	tele**phon**e sym**phon**y	_____
self-	oneself	**self**-image **self**less	_____
auto-	self	**auto**graph **auto**matic	_____

2. Complete the sentences with one of the above words.

a. The _____ was wonderful. They played Bach and Hayden.

b. I don't have to change gears in my car. It's an _____.

c. I am studying to be a psychologist so _____ communication is very important for me to learn about.

d. He never thinks about himself and he's always giving to other people. He is really _____.

e. Last night was very clear, so I took my _____ outside and looked at the stars.

f. The damage from the earthquake was immediately _____. Buildings fell down and fires began. It was a terrible sight.

g. I have a friend who collects _____s of famous people.

h. He is very intelligent, but he has a negative _____. He doesn't feel secure about himself at all.

Look Back

A. Vocabulary

DIRECTIONS: Circle the letter of the choice that best completes each sentence.

1. The man studied in the field for thirty-five years. He is a _____ in the field.

   a. counselor   b. newcomer   c. specialist

2. I was certainly surprised when I heard the news. I was _____.

   a. shocked   b. bored   c. accustomed to it

3. Childhood is the first _____ of a person's life. Or is it the second?

   a. stage   b. image   c. impression

4. I collect stamps. That is my _____.

   a. development   b. hobby   c. source

5. My first _____ of the airport was terrible.

   a. impression   b. newness   c. alternative

6. Some medicine makes people feel tired and _____.

   a. homesick   b. familiar   c. disoriented

7. He was born in Kentucky. He is a _____ of Kentucky.

   a. native   b. newcomer   c. term

8. There is a good _____ feeling in our neighborhood. We all help each other.

   a. custom   b. self-conscious   c. community

9. I have to find a _____ for this problem.

   a. stage   b. custom   c. solution

10. He imagined that people were trying to kill him. He was very _____.

    a. successful   b. paranoid   c. established

B. Matching

DIRECTIONS: *Find the word or phrase in column B which has a similar mean-*
ing to a word in column A. Write the letter of that word or
phrase next to the word in column A.

	A		B
1.	_____ image	a.	say again
2.	_____ unfamiliar	b.	assistance
3.	_____ repeat	c.	easy
4.	_____ service	d.	change a little
5.	_____ fear	e.	stranger
6.	_____ environment	f.	strange
7.	_____ newcomer	g.	fright
8.	_____ adjust	h.	very sad
9.	_____ simple	i.	area around you
10.	_____ depressed	j.	picture

C. Synthesis Questions

Find someone who has visited another country (your country, if possible). Find out what was the most difficult thing he or she experienced
there. Find out if he or she experienced culture shock in that country or
when he or she returned to his or her own country.

D. Vocabulary Preview

DIRECTIONS: *What shorter words can you see in these words from Chapter 6?*

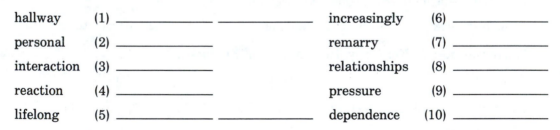

hallway	(1) _____ _____	increasingly	(6) _____
personal	(2) _____	remarry	(7) _____
interaction	(3) _____	relationships	(8) _____
reaction	(4) _____	pressure	(9) _____
lifelong	(5) _____ _____	dependence	(10) _____

Contemporary American Society

section 1

A First Look

A. Background Building

1. Look at the illustration on the preceding page. Write some differences you see between the family in the picture on the wall and the family on TV.

        FAMILY IN PICTURE   FAMILY ON TV

2. What does this illustration show you about American society?

3. Complete these sentences about your hometown. You may have more than one answer.

   a. I come from _____.

      a. a town   b. a small city   c. a large city

   b. My family has lived there for _____.

      a. less than   b. my whole life   c. many generations
        five years

   c. Most of the people in my town/city know me _____.

      a. very well   b. a little   c. not well at all

   d. On the street, in my city/town, I say hello to most of the people I see.

      a. yes   b. no

   e. For entertainment, most people in my town/city _____.

      a. stay in town   b. go to another town or city

4. Complete these sentences about life in your country.

   a. Divorce is _____ in my country.

      a. common   b. fairly common   c. uncommon

   b. Young men and women _____ live together before they get married.

      a. often   b. sometimes   c. never

c. Parents _____ want their children to be independent.

      a. do   b. don't

5. What is a question you have about American society? Write it here.

Find the answer by reading this chapter and asking your teacher and other people.

B. Topic

DIRECTIONS: Before you begin to read, look at these topics. There is one topic for each paragraph. Look quickly at the reading to find these topics. Do not read every word at this point. Write the number of the paragraph next to the topic of that paragraph.

1. _____ a transient society

2. _____ marriage and divorce

3. _____ life for young people now

4. _____ traditional life in a small town

5. _____ bringing up children

C. Reading

DIRECTIONS: Now read.

	1
In the past fifty years, American society has changed a great	1
deal. Fifty years ago, most Americans lived in small communities.	2
They rarely moved from one area to another and usually knew their	3
neighbors at least by name if not by close, personal interaction. Life	4
was so personal in those days that people often joked about it. They	5
said that a person could not even stay home from church on Sunday	6
without the whole town knowing about it. It was difficult to have	7
privacy in a small community like that, but there was usually a	8
sense of security, of belonging, and of community togetherness in	9
such places. Except for church and the local movie theater, there	10
was not much in the way of entertainment. Some people dreamed	11
about moving to the exciting life of the big cities, but most people	12
were happy to live all their lives in the same community.	13
Few people experience this type of lifelong social interaction	14
or sense of community togetherness now. Contemporary American	15
society is much more transient now; people often move from neigh-	16
borhood to neighborhood, city to city, and coast to coast. It is rare	17
to find people who have lived all their lives in one community. Be-	18

1   In the past fifty years, American society has changed a great deal. Fifty years ago, most Americans lived in small communities. They rarely moved from one area to another and usually knew their neighbors at least by name if not by close, personal interaction. Life was so personal in those days that people often joked about it. They said that a person could not even stay home from church on Sunday without the whole town knowing about it. It was difficult to have privacy in a small community like that, but there was usually a sense of security, of belonging, and of community togetherness in such places. Except for church and the local movie theater, there was not much in the way of entertainment. Some people dreamed about moving to the exciting life of the big cities, but most people were happy to live all their lives in the same community.

   Few people experience this type of lifelong social interaction or sense of community togetherness now. Contemporary American society is much more transient now; people often move from neighborhood to neighborhood, city to city, and coast to coast. It is rare to find people who have lived all their lives in one community. Be-

2

cause people move so frequently, they do not have a chance to get
to know their neighbors. Perhaps this is also why Americans tend
to have a more casual attitude about friendships than people from
some other cultures; Americans are accustomed to leaving friends
and making new friends. In this impersonal society, they have lost
the habit of saying hello to people they pass on the streets or in the
hallways of their apartment buildings.

3

The American family has also gone through many changes in
the past fifty years. Primary among these changes is the current
attitude about divorce, the legal end of a marriage. Until the 1960s,
divorce was quite uncommon. However, between 1962 and 1981, the
number of divorces each year tripled. With less emphasis on tradition, on religion, and on the economic dependence of women on
men (due to the increase of women who work), Americans seem less
likely to remain in a marriage that has problems. They are not forced
by economic, social, or religious pressure to stay married. Partly as
a reaction to the high divorce rate, many Americans live together
without being married. They feel that it is a good idea to know each
other well before they become legally tied. This is particularly common in the more liberal areas of the country—the East and West
Coasts and the large cities of the North.

4

Since the 1960s, both the number of single-parent families and
the number of mothers who work outside the home have doubled.
Obviously, children have greater responsibilities in these nontraditional families. However, bringing up children to be independent
has always been a part of the American culture. At an early age
American children learn to do things on their own. They learn to
take care of themselves by cleaning their rooms, helping with the
dishes and the laundry, and spending time away from their parents,
either in daycare, with a babysitter, or alone. Older children often
do work for other people such as babysitting or cutting the grass.
Most teenagers try to find summer or after-school jobs so that they
can have their own spending money. While in college young people
usually work part time and during summer vacations in a variety of
jobs ranging from construction work to waiting on tables in restaurants.

5

In the past, most young people moved away from home when
they finished high school, either to go to college or to get a job and
live with friends. Now, however, the cost of living is so high that
many people under 25 are moving back in with their parents. Young
people are getting married later now than they used to: the average
age for a woman to get married is now about 24 and, for a man, 26.
Nowadays, newly married couples often postpone having children
while they are establishing careers. Once they have children, they
face difficult decisions about whether the mother should continue
working and, if so, who should care for the children.

19
20
21
22
23
24
25
26
27
28
29
30
31
32
33
34
35
36
37
38
39
40
41
42
43
44
45
46
47
48
49
50
51
52
53
54
55
56
57
58
59
60
61
62
63
64

Underline an idea in the reading that you think is surprising. Talk to your classmates about this idea.

D. Scanning/Vocabulary

Part 1

DIRECTIONS: Write the line number where you find the word(s). Then choose the best
meaning for the word as it is used in that sentence.

1. interaction   line number _____

    a. person to person   b. greeting   c. reaction
    contact

2. belonging   line number _____

    a. being a part of   b. owned   c. missing

3. togetherness   line number _____

    a. feeling close   b. living   c. ownership

4. contemporary   line number _____

    a. person of same age   b. modern   c. ordered by time

5. casual   line number _____

    a. easy-going   b. formal   c. serious

6. primary   line number _____

    a. at an early age   b. basic color   c. of first importance

7. remain   line number _____

    a. stay   b. finish   c. end

8. reaction   line number _____

    a. response   b. reason   c. chemical change

9. teenagers   line number _____

    a. young children   b. students   c. older children

10. face   line number _____

    a. front of a building   b. have in front of them   c. the front of the head

Part 2

DIRECTIONS: Find a word that is the opposite of the one given. The line where you will find the word is given.

1. line 3   often   _____
2. line 9   danger   _____
3. line 16   staying in one place   _____
4. line 23   personal   _____
5. line 29   common   _____
6. line 30   decreased   _____
7. line 38   conservative   _____
8. line 42   traditional   _____

E. Reading Comprehension

DIRECTIONS: Circle the letter of the choice that best completes each sentence.

1. Fifty years ago, Americans moved around _____.

   a. a lot
   b. from one area to another
   c. less than they do now

2. The author states that more mothers work outside the home now in _____.

   a. single-parent families
   b. general
   c. two-parent families

3. Single-parent families are _____.

   a. always single-parent families
   b. more common now than before
   c. three times as numerous as before

4. In lines 42–43, "nontraditional families" means _____.

   a. single-parent families
   b. families with the mother working
   c. both a and b

5. People probably _____ went to church when they lived in small communities.

   a. rarely
   b. often
   c. sometimes

6. People today _____ live all their lives in one community in the United States.

   a. almost never
   b. usually
   c. almost always

7. The author thinks that Americans and people from other cultures have _____ ideas about friendships.

    a. similar

    b. strange

    c. different

8. In paragraph 3, the author mentions _____ things that used to make divorce difficult.

    a. three

    b. four

    c. seven

9. Fifty years ago, children _____.

    a. had greater responsibilities

    b. were probably independent also

    c. were not very independent

10. When people get married now, they probably _____.

    a. have more children

    b. live with his parents

    c. wait to have children

Look Again

A. Vocabulary

DIRECTIONS: Circle the letter of the choice that best completes each sentence.

1. People come and go here all the time. It is really a very _____ community.

    a. misleading   b. transient   c. dependent

2. I never have coffee _____ sugar.

    a. unless   b. in spite of   c. without

3. Business letters are usually very _____.

    a. private   b. impersonal   c. pressured

4. A large salary generally gives people financial _____.

    a. security   b. statistics   c. assistance

5. I like that class because the teacher _____ grammar rules and I need to understand grammar more clearly.

    a. interacts   b. postpones   c. emphasizes

6. I don't know them very well. We are just _____ friends.

    a. personal   b. casual   c. temporary

7. This magazine is over a year old. The news in it isn't _____.

    a. tripled   b. current   c. casual

8. A _____ is something I do without thinking. I am accustomed to it.

    a. tradition   b. habit   c. reaction

9. They did not associate with each other. They had little _____.

    a. dependence   b. personality   c. interaction

10. There was an emergency so we had to _____ our meeting.

    a. postpone   b. establish   c. bring up

B. Reading Comprehension

DIRECTIONS: Complete the following summary of the reading. Try to answer in your own words without looking back at the reading.

Paragraph 1: Introduction

Fifty years ago, people lived in (1) _____ towns. People (2) _____ their neighbors well.

Paragraph 2

In contrast, American society is (3) _____ now because (4) _____.

Paragraph 3

A major change in American society: (5) _____
Some reasons why divorce is more common: less emphasis on
(6) _____, (7) _____, and
(8) _____ dependence of women on men.
As a reaction to high divorce rates, (9) _____
_____.

Paragraph 4

(10) _____.
Examples: young children help clean up and spend time with babysitters; older children and teenagers earn money by working for other people.

Paragraph 5

Young people are moving back home with their parents because (11) _____.
They are getting married (12) _____. They have to make difficult decisions about having (13) _____ and whether or not the (14) _____ should work.

C. Think About It

1. Were you surprised by any information in the reading? What? Explain it to a classmate.

2. How do you think community life is different in your culture from community life in the United States?

3. How do you think atittudes about friendships are different in your culture from attitudes in the United States?

4. In the United States, working parents have to find someone to take care of their children while they work. Some daycare possibilities are:

   a. children stay at home and someone comes in to take care of them;

   b. children go to another home where someone takes care of them as well as other children;

   c. children go to a daycare center where professionals take care of them.

   Do people in your country need daycare for their children? Explain why or why not.

5. Why do you think people live together before they are married?

D. Reading

DIRECTIONS: Read and answer the questions below.

Jack and May Young work at a factory. Jack works days (7 a.m. to 4 p.m.), but May alternates between the day shift and the night shift (4 p.m. to 1 a.m.). They have two children, Anna, 9, and Justin, 6. After thirteen years of marriage, Jack has moved out and asked May for a divorce. May doesn't know for sure, but she thinks that Jack is going to move in with a co-worker, a woman with two young children.

May doesn't want a divorce so this situation is very difficult for her, but, to make matters worse, Jack says that he wants custody of the children. He knows that May is a good mother, but he thinks that he can take better care of them because he will be home when they are at home.

1. Is May ever at home when the children are not in school?

2. Does Jack have a girlfriend?

3. Who do you think should have custody of the children? Why?

Contact a Point of View

A. Background Building

DIRECTIONS: Answer the following questions.

1. When you were a teenager, how did you spend your free time?

2. Did you spend most of your time at your own house, at friends' houses, or out?

3. Do/Did your parents worry about you?

B. Timed Reading

DIRECTIONS: Read the following point of view and answer the questions in four minutes.

My name is Ron Perotta. I have three teenagers, two girls and a boy. I want to tell you it's not easy to have kids nowadays. They all laugh because I'm always saying, "When I was a kid. . . ." But, it's true; when I was a kid, things were different. Families were closer. We all went to church together. I make my family go to church every Sunday, but we are the only ones in our neighborhood who go. So my kids think that religion is just another one of Dad's traditional ideas. There is not much support for traditional ideas nowadays.

It's hard to be a parent these days. My parents never had to worry about drugs, about sex, about the danger for their kids on the street. Kids weren't even supposed to know about sex, unless they lived on a farm, until they were sixteen or so. There were some problems, I guess, even then, but there weren't as many. Drugs and violence weren't all around us like they are now.

Well, I'm a realist. I expect my kids will probably try marijuana and alcohol and my girls may live with their boyfriends. I won't like it and I'll fight to prevent it, but that's the way it is. But I think that basically my kids are good kids. I think they'll grow up and get married. They'll probably have the same kinds of values that my wife and I have. I just wish it were 1965 again. Those were the good old days!

DIRECTIONS: *Read each of the following statements carefully to determine whether each is true (T), false (F), or impossible to know (ITK).*

1. _____ The writer is a mother.

2. _____ Ron has six children.

3. _____ Ron's neighbors go to church every Sunday.

4. _____ Drugs, sex, and violence were big problems when Ron was young.

5. _____ Kids who lived on a farm were supposed to know about sex.

6. _____ Ron thinks it is a good idea for people to live together without being married.

7. _____ Ron thinks that traditional ideas are unpopular now.

8. _____ Ron's children tried marijuana last year.

9. _____ Ron thinks that religion is important.

10. _____ Ron is married.

C. Vocabulary

DIRECTIONS: *Circle the letter of the word(s) with the same meaning as the italicized word(s).*

1. We have five *kids*.

   a. parents   b. relatives   c. children

2. It's *hard* to be a parent.

    a. difficult   b. single   c. busy

3. I can't *prevent* my friend from moving.

    a. stop   b. follow   c. develop

4. I am *worried* about my children.

    a. angry   b. concerned   c. idealistic

5. What *kind* of ice cream do you have?

    a. product   b. area   c. type

6. The PTA is the *Parent*-Teacher Association.

    a. child   b. father or mother   c. president

7. They seem to *grow up* too quickly.

    a. become adults   b. take drugs   c. continue

8. In *those days* I felt like a different person.

    a. another place   b. the past   c. postwar times

9. What *else* do you want to do today?

    a. time   b. important   c. other thing

10. Will you *support* me with this new idea?

    a. prevent   b. help   c. show

D. React

DIRECTIONS: Answer the following questions and then share your answers with a classmate or with the class.

1. Which three of the following worries do parents have most about their children in your country?

    _____ physical danger

    _____ education

    _____ drugs

    _____ premarital sex

    _____ loss of religion

    _____ extreme religions

    _____ alcohol

_____ teenage pregnancy

_____ kidnapping

_____ violence outside the home

_____ violence inside the home

_____ teenage suicide

OTHER PROBLEMS

_____ _____

_____ _____

_____ _____

_____ _____

2. Now decide the three most difficult problems for parents today in the U.S.

3. In the United States, teenagers usually go through a stage that is very difficult as they try to establish their independence from their parents. Is this "rebellious" stage common in your country?

4. Some parents and teenagers get along better than others. What do you think makes the difference?

E. Word Analysis

Part 1

DIRECTIONS: _Look at the endings for_ verbs _and_ adjectives. _Are the italicized words in the sentences verbs or adjectives?_

VERBS	**ADJECTIVES**
like	lik*able*
accept	accept*able*

	VERB	ADJECTIVE
1. Ask anyone. Everyone here is very *knowledgeable*.	_____	_____
2. Her personality *changes* like the wind.	_____	_____
3. That solution is *unthinkable*.	_____	_____
4. What do Americans *value?*	_____	_____
5. He usually has very *changeable* ideas.	_____	_____

	VERB	ADJECTIVE

6. *Compare* the two cars. They are very similar. _____ _____

7. This is a very strange place; the weather *changes* almost every hour. _____ _____

8. Your decision is not *workable*. _____ _____

9. Those two cars have *comparable* engines. _____ _____

10. I know what you mean. It's *understandable*. _____ _____

Part 2

1. Study the meanings of these: Another example: _____

trans-	across	transportation transient	_____
port-	carry	transport export	_____
ex-, e-	out of, from	export emigrate	_____
im-,	into	import immigrate	_____
tri-	three	triple tripod	_____
bi-	two	binoculars bilingual	_____
temp-	time	contemporary tempo	_____
mono-	one	monogamy	_____
poly-	many	polygamy	_____

2. Complete the sentences with one of the above words.

a. They study in two languages at school. It is a _____ school.

b. When did your parents _____ to the United States?

c. A big problem in some countries is that the well-educated people _____ _____ from those countries instead of staying and contributing what they can to the society.

d. A trading company _____ and _____
   things from one country to another.

e. I brought my _____ so I can see everything up close.

f. John Kennedy and Martin Luther King lived at the same time. They were
   _____(s).

g. Professional photographers stand their cameras on _____(s).

h. You are only supposed to have one wife in the U.S. _____
   is the law. In some cultures you can have more than one wife. _____
   is permitted.

Look Back

A. Vocabulary

DIRECTIONS: Circle the letter of the choice that best completes each sentence.

1. It increased from 50 to 150. The number _____.

   a. declined   b. doubled   c. tripled

2. I know my friend is a little crazy sometimes, but _____ he is a good person.

   a. early   b. in relationships   c. basically

3. A lot of people live in my house and there is very little _____. I can't get away from the other people to be by myself.

   a. privacy   b. noise   c. socializing

4. There is too much crime and _____ on television shows today. I think it has a bad influence on children and on adults, too.

   a. divorce   b. privacy   c. violence

5. In the afternoon a babysitter comes in to _____ the children.

   a. raise   b. grow up   c. take care of

6. What is your _____ reason for coming here?

   a. primary   b. previous   c realistic

7. In the _____ world, TV is an important means of communication.

   a. contemporary   b. statistical   c. violent

8. This writer always _____ descriptions of scenery. I like more action.

   a. prevents   b. emphasizes   c. reshapes

9. I'm sorry, but I'm going to have to _____ our meeting. Could you come back on Wednesday?

   a. face   b. establish   c. postpone

10. We always celebrate our holidays in the _____ way.

   a. traditional   b. supportive   c. experienced

B. Matching

DIRECTIONS: Find the word or phrase in column B which has a similar mean-ing to a word in column A. Write the letter of that word or phrase next to the word in column A.

	A		B
1.	_____ prevent	a.	wait to do later
2.	_____ neighborhood	b.	repeated action requiring no thought
3.	_____ habit		
4.	_____ primary	c.	closeness
5.	_____ town	d.	typical
6.	_____ togetherness	e.	stop before it happens
7.	_____ sense	f.	area of places to live
8.	_____ establish	g.	set up
9.	_____ postpone	h.	major
10.	_____ common	i.	feeling
		j.	very small city

C. Synthesis Questions

DIRECTIONS: Answer the following questions.

1. Discuss the changes in your country's society in the past fifty years. Talk about general changes as well as changes in family life.

2. Choose some aspect of American life (for example, education, bringing up children, crime). Work with a classmate to develop questions about this topic. Interview people and report back to the class.

D. Vocabulary Preview

What shorter words can you find in these words?

Protestant   (1) _____

percentage   (2) _____

lifestyles   (3) _____

useless	(4)	_____
assistance	(5)	_____
retirees	(6)	_____
productive	(7)	_____
retirement	(8)	_____
carefully	(9)	_____
employer	(10)	_____
government	(11)	_____
employees	(12)	_____

What does the "ees" at the end of the retirees and employees mean? How is employer different from employee? (13) _____

chapter 7

Retirement

A First Look

A. Background Building

1. Look at the illustration on the previous page and answer the questions below.

   a. What are these two people doing?

   b. Do you think that they are on vacation?

   c. How old do you think they are?

   d. "Retire" means to stop working when you are old. What do you think a "retirement city" is?

2. Complete these sentences about your culture.

   a. People usually retire when they are _____.

   b. After retirement, they spend their time _____ing
                                              (verb)

B. Topic

DIRECTIONS: *Before you begin to read, look at these topics. There is one topic for each paragraph. Look quickly at the reading to find these topics. Do not read every word at this point. Write the number of the paragraph next to the topic of that paragraph.*

1. _____ the financial problems of retirement

2. _____ the value of work in America

3. _____ answers to some problems

4. _____ the positive side of retirement

5. _____ explanation of retirement

C. Reading

DIRECTIONS: Now read.

1

Work is a very important part of life in the United States. 1
When the early Protestant immigrants came to this country, they 2
brought the idea that work was the way to God and heaven. This 3
attitude, the Protestant work ethic, still influences America today. 4
Work is not only important for economic benefits, the salary, but 5
also for social and psychological needs, the feeling of doing some- 6
thing for the good of the society. Americans spend most of their 7
lives working, being productive. For most Americans, their work 8
defines them: They are what they do. What happens, then, when a 9
person can no longer work? 10

2

Most Americans stop working at age sixty-five or seventy and 11
retire. Because work is such an important part of life in this culture, 12
retirement can be very difficult. Retirees often feel that they are 13
useless and unproductive. Of course, some people are happy to re- 14
tire; but leaving one's job, whatever it is, is a difficult change, even 15
for those who look forward to retiring. Many retirees do not know 16
how to use their time or they feel lost without their jobs. 17

3

Retirement can also bring financial problems. Many people 18
rely on Social Security checks every month. During their working 19
years, employees contribute a certain percentage of their salaries 20
to the government. Each employer also gives a certain percentage 21
to the government. When people retire, they receive this money as 22
income. These checks do not provide enough money to live on, how- 23
ever, because prices are increasing very rapidly. Senior citizens, 24
those over sixty-five, have to have savings in the bank or other re- 25
tirement plans to make ends meet. The rate of inflation is forcing 26
prices higher each year; Social Security checks alone cannot cover 27
these growing expenses. The government offers some assistance, 28
Medicare (health care) and welfare (general assistance), but many 29
senior citizens have to change their lifestyles after retirement. They 30
have to spend carefully to be sure that they can afford to buy food, 31
fuel, and other necessities. 32

4

Of course, many senior citizens are happy with retirement. 33
They have time to spend with their families or to enjoy their hob- 34
bies. Some continue to work part time; others do volunteer work. 35
Some, like those in the Retired Business Executives Association, 36
even help young people to get started in new businesses. Many re- 37
tired citizens also belong to "Golden Age" groups. These organi- 38
zations plan trips and social events. There are many opportunities 39
for retirees. 40

5

American society is only beginning to be concerned about the 41
special physical and emotional needs of its senior citizens. The gov- 42

ernment is taking steps to ease the problem of limited income. They 43
are building new housing, offering discounts in stores and museums 44
and on buses, and providing other services, such as free courses, 45
food service, and help with housework. Retired citizens are a rapidly 46
growing percentage of the population. This part of the population 47
is very important and we must respond to their needs. After all, 48
every citizen will be a senior citizen some day. 49

React

Underline one interesting idea from the reading. Read it
aloud several times to yourself to understand its meaning
more fully.

D. Scanning/Vocabulary

Part 1

DIRECTIONS: Write the line number where you find the word(s). Then choose the best
meaning for the word as it is used in that sentence.

1. work   line number _____
   a. material   b. jobs   c. business

2. influences   line number _____
   a. changes   b. affects   c. compares

3. economic   line number _____
   a. partial   b. financial   c. supportive

4. productive   line number _____
   a. useful   b. unnecessary   c. professional

5. retirement   line number _____
   a. stopping work   b. employment   c. taking a rest

6. employer   line number _____
   a. worker   b. boss   c. businessman

7. afford   line number _____
   a. be able to buy   b. contribute   c. prevents

8. volunteer   line number _____

   a. unpaid   b. salaried   c. intentional

9. contribute   line number _____

   a. include   b. take   c. give

10. provide   line number _____

   a. give   b. prepare   c. offer

Part 2

DIRECTIONS: Find a word in the reading which has a meaning similar to the following. The line is given.

1. belief (4)   _____

2. pay (5)   _____

3. useful (8)   _____

4. unimportant (14)   _____

5. depend on (19)   _____

6. part (21)   _____

7. salary (23)   _____

8. needed things (32)   _____

9. older (33)   _____

10. worried (41)   _____

11. reduced prices (44)   _____

12. answer (48)   _____

E. Reading Comprehension

DIRECTIONS: Circle the letter of the choice that best completes each sentence.

1. The author believes that work first became important to Americans because of _____ pressure.

   a. economic   b. religious   c. family

2. Protestants believed in _____.

   a. high salaries   b. America   c. hard work

3. Senior citizens have to have other savings because Social Security checks _____.

   a. are not enough

   b. come monthly

   c. cover growing expenses

4. When Americans stop work, it is difficult for them to _____.

   a. feel productive

   b. get Social Security checks

   c. be religious

5. According to the author, _____ Americans stop work at age sixty-five or seventy.

   a. some

   b. a few

   c. most

6. The author mentions _____ examples of discounts.

   a. two

   b. three

   c. four

7. Many retirees feel useless because they _____.

   a. do volunteer work

   b. have limited incomes

   c. aren't working

8. The last sentence of the reading means that each person _____.

   a. is important

   b. is a citizen

   c. will grow old

9. A salary is a _____ benefit.

   a. psychological

   b. social

   c. financial

10. Many people who retire feel unproductive because their work _____.

   a. defined their lives

   b. was unimportant

   c. was difficult

Look Again

A. Vocabulary

DIRECTIONS: Circle the letter of the choice that best completes each sentence.

1. Clothing is an example of a(n) _____.

   a. assistance   b. necessity   c. concern

2. It is very late. She is very _____ about her son.

   a. productive   b. demanding   c. concerned

3. My _____ pays me a good salary.

   a. volunteer   b. employer   c. employee

4. Every year I _____ a percentage of my income to my church.

   a. limit   b. receive   c. contribute

5. Every year he _____ to work at the school; he never gets paid.

   a. gets by   b. volunteers   c. provides

6. The older children in a family always _____ the younger ones.

   a. establish   b. influence   c. define

7. I don't have enough money to buy a new car. I cannot _____ one.

   a. demand   b. provide   c. afford

8. Your salary is very low. Do you have any other _____?

   a. income   b. interest   c. percentage

9. His physical condition is unbelievable: he's seventy and he _____ jogs.

   a. no longer   b. then   c. still

10. He is a _____ volunteer here at the hospital; he is a big problem and no help.

    a. productive   b. useful   c. useless

B. Vocabulary/Comprehension

DIRECTIONS: *Complete the reading summary with the words from this list. Try to complete it first without looking back at the reading.*

retirement	relax	free
work	productive	useless
sixty-five	important	retire
hobby		

Generally speaking, Americans (1) _____ until they are (2) _____. Then they (3) _____. (4) _____ can be very difficult for people because their work was so (5) _____ to them. Often people work so much that they do not take the time to (6) _____ or to have a(n) (7) _____. Then when they retire, they don't know what to do with all the (8) _____ time on their hands. They also can feel (9) _____ because they are not being (10) _____. Retirement isn't easy.

C. Think About It

1. One problem for senior citizens is financial. List some sources of income that retirees in the U.S. have.

2. Does your country have a social security system similar to the one in the United States? How does the system work? Do senior citizens have enough money to live on?

3. Another problem that retirees face is what to do with all their free time. What are some of the activities mentioned in the reading?

4. What do you think are the most serious problems of old age? Write #1 next to the most serious problem for the elderly.

In your home country

_____ financial   _____ physical   _____ psychological   _____ housing

In the United States

_____ financial   _____ physical   _____ psychological   _____ housing

D. Graph

DIRECTIONS: The question of growing old is different for different countries. Study the following chart and answer the questions below.

Estimated population in selected countries for the year 1990.

	MEDIAN AGE*	PERCENTAGE OF POPULATION FROM AGE 0–14	PERCENTAGE OF POPULATION 65 AND OLDER
Australia	31.8	22.5	10.8
Brazil	22.7	35.2	4.7
France	38.5	19.2	13.0
Greece	36.5	21.1	13.4
Ghana	16.5	47.1	2.8
Indonesia	22.0	35.7	3.8
Japan	36.8	19.2	11.4
Korea	24.1	32.4	4.2
Lebanon	21.5	35.3	5.1
Malaysia	21.9	35.7	3.9
Mexico	19.6	39.1	3.7
Sweden	39.0	16.0	17.6
Switzerland	38.1	16.6	14.8
U.S.S.R.	31.5	25.1	9.4
U.S.	32.8	22.1	12.2
Venezuela	20.8	38.3	3.7

*median age means that 50 percent of the population is older than that age and 50 percent is younger.
Source: World Population Prospectus: Estimates and Projections as Assessed in 1984. New York: United Nations, 1986.

There are great differences in the age of the populations in the various countries.

1. Which country has the largest percentage of retired people? _____

2. Which country has the largest percentage of children? _____

3. In which country is more than 50 percent of the population over 39? _____

4. Find two countries which have similar population trends? Explain why.

   a. _____

   b. _____

If these population trends continue, think about what will happen in different countries, and how the number of older people and the number of children will affect life in those countries.

Contact a Point of View

A. Background Building

Read these two opinions about retirement. Which is more positive? Which do you think your parents will have when they retire? How about you?

1. "I've never been happier. I finally have time to do all the things that I had always wanted to do."

2. "I have too much time and I don't always know what to do with myself. I almost never see my friends from work."

B. Timed Reading

DIRECTIONS: *Read the following point of view and answer the questions in four minutes.*

I retired about a year ago. The company had a big party for me and gave me a gold watch for more than thirty years of service. At the party, everyone said to me, "Retirement is a time to do all the things you didn't have time to do. It's a new beginning." I can't say that I dislike retirement, but after working for thirty-five years, day after day, it's hard to adjust to all this free time.

Just after I retired, Peg and I went to visit John, Jr. in Chicago and Ann in New York. We really had a good time. We enjoy being together. In fact, John, Jr. invited us to come and live with him. He knows that living on Social Security checks and a small retirement plan is not easy. But we decided not to move in with him. We have our lives and he and his wife have theirs. We are going to stay here in town. We may move to an apartment, because the house is too big for only the two of us and it's hard to keep clean. Peg is having some trouble with her back; she's seeing the doctor tomorrow.

Money isn't a serious problem for us because we do have some savings, but we have to make careful decisions about what we can afford. We're not used to living on a fixed income, but we make ends meet. I still belong to the club and I play cards there once a week, and we spend time with other retired couples in the area. My only regret is that I didn't spend enough time thinking about retirement before it happened.

DIRECTIONS: *Read each of the following statements carefully to determine whether each is true (T), false (F), or impossible to know (ITK).*

1. _____ This man retired about six months ago.

2. _____ The people at the party were negative about retiring.

3. _____ This man's son is married.

4. _____ This man worked for forty years in the company.

5. _____ He and his wife are moving in with John, Jr.

6. _____ This man dislikes retirement.

7. _____ He and his wife live only on their savings and a retirement plan.

8. _____ This man has other children at home.

9. _____ This man has some physical problems.

10. _____ This man and his wife are going to move from the town.

C. Vocabulary

DIRECTIONS: *Fill in the blanks with vocabulary from the reading. Make necessary changes in the form of the word.*

1. serious/regret/plans

   I have some _____ _____ about my

   _____ to live away from my family.

2. in fact/begin/back/trouble

   Little by little he is _____ to feel better. _____,

   he has no _____ at all with his _____ now.

3. dislike/decisions/money

   I _____ making _____ about _____.

4. limited/afford/make ends meet

   I can't _____ to live on a _____ income be-

   cause I can't _____.

D. React

DIRECTIONS: Show your opinion of the following statements by putting 1 next to your first preference, 2 next to your second choice, and so on through 6. Share your ideas with a classmate or the class.

When my parents grow old and retire, I hope that they live

_____ with me.

_____ with my brother.

_____ with my sister.

_____ some time with me, and some time with my brother and/or sister.

_____ near me, so I can visit them.

_____ independently of the family.

Often a real problem happens when one parent dies and the other is alone. If my father died, I'm sure that my mother would

_____ continue living where she is living.

_____ move in with me.

_____ live with my brother.

_____ live with my sister.

_____ move to a smaller residence.

_____ move to a nursing home (a home for the elderly).

E. Word Analysis

Part 1

DIRECTIONS: *Choose the appropriate word form in each sentence.*

1. special
   specialty

2. pain
   painful
   painless

3. simple
   simplicity

4. knowledge
   knowledgeable

5. beneficial
   benefit

6. cultural
   culture

7. familiarity
   familiar

8. fear
   fearless
   fearful

9. impressionable
   impression

10. senseless
    sense

1. What is the _____ of this restaurant?

2. What a _____ in the neck!

3. She is a _____ child.

4. Her _____ of physics surprised me.

5. It is _____ to visit another country.

6. Differences in _____ often cause serious trouble.

7. I was unaccustomed to the _____ in that society.

8. He is without _____ .

9. She is very young and _____ .

10. What is the real _____ of this word?

Part 2

1. Study the meanings of these:

			Another example:
-er	the subject of the stem	trainer	_____
-ee	the object of the stem	trainee	_____

(Note: -er endings are more common than -ee endings)

popul-	people	**population**	_____
cent-	hundred	**percentage**	_____
psych-	the mind	**psychological**	_____

2. Complete the sentences with one of the above words.

   a. What is the _____ of your city?

   b. Sometimes retirement is a big _____ adjustment. It takes
      time to get used to it.

   c. In the circus, an animal _____ works very closely with the
      animal to teach it tricks.

   d. What _____ of the people voted against gun control?

   e. My sister is a _____ in computer programming. She's learn-
      ing a lot in her program.

3. Write the meaning of the boldfaced word on the line.

   a. The city celebrated its **bicentennial** with a parade and other special activities.

      _____

   b. The man tried to kill his family. He was **psychotic**.

      _____

   c. The **manager** showed the **trainees** around the store.

      _____ _____

   d. The law was extremely **unpopular**. _____

Look Back

A. Vocabulary

DIRECTIONS: Circle the letter of the choice that best completes each sentence.

1. Poverty in a wealthy society is a(n) _____ problem.

   a. mobile   b. ethical   c. spacious

2. She is in her last year of high school. She is a _____.

   a. junior   b. senior   c. beginner

3. A car is a(n) _____ in the suburbs.

   a. aspect   b. establishment   c. necessity

4. Don't worry. Everything will be fine. Heaven will _____.

   a. produce   b. provide   c. make ends meet

5. This coat is _____. You can have it with 15 percent off.

   a. salaried   b. increasing   c. discounted

6. The price of gold _____ daily.

   a. costs   b. inflates   c. develops

7. I can _____ with twenty dollars a day.

   a. afford   b. make ends meet   c. look for

8. This hat is _____ in the rain. It's too small and doesn't cover my head.

   a. fixed   b. useless   c. casual

9. Our culture _____ our thoughts and actions.

   a. influences   b. gets started   c. contains

10. He's a very good student. _____, he's the best in the class.

    a. For example   b. In fact   c. Therefore

B. Matching

DIRECTIONS: *Find the word or phrase in column B which has a similar meaning to a word in column A. Write the letter of that word or phrase next to the word in column A.*

	A		B
1.	_____ afford	a.	useful
2.	_____ provide	b.	affect
3.	_____ necessities	c.	value
4.	_____ influence	d.	part
5.	_____ ethic	e.	needed things
6.	_____ financial	f.	be able to buy
7.	_____ growing	g.	economic
8.	_____ percentage	h.	respond
9.	_____ answer	i.	increasing
10.	_____ productive	j.	give

C. Synthesis Questions

1. Visit a retirement community or an old age home. Work with your teacher to arrange your visit. Some possibilities: prepare some entertainment for the people there; become a "conversation partner" with someone there; prepare some snacks for some of the people there and have some informal discussions with them; ask to interview them about questions you have prepared.

2. A recent study about old age showed that older people were happy with their lives but that young people thought that senior citizens were lonely and worried. Think about a senior citizen you know. Is that person lonely or unhappy? What does this person do with his or her free time?

3. The United States is often criticized for being a country where everyone wants to be young, especially older people. Think about older people you have seen in the United States. Write some positive aspects of their lives and some negative aspects:

   Positive   Negative

4. There is a well-known expression in English: "You're only as old as you feel." What do you think this means? Do you agree?

D. Vocabulary Preview

DIRECTIONS: What smaller words can you find in the following words?

equalize	(1) _____		wealthy	(7) _____
differences	(2) _____		upper	(8) _____
successful	(3) _____		royalty	(9) _____
equality	(4) _____		background	(10) _____
restrooms	(5) _____		powerful	(11) _____
protection	(6) _____		minority	(12) _____

E. Skimming

DIRECTIONS: Look quickly at the next page. Answer these questions.

1. What book is this from?
2. What information is listed?

F. Scanning

Answer these questions as quickly as possible.

3. Find an organization that helps seniors with health problems.
4. Find three organizations that help seniors get good food to eat.
5. Find an organization that helps a senior who cannot drive.
6. Find an organization that helps Indochinese and Chinese senior citizens.
7. Where can seniors go if they want people to socialize with?
8. What is your reaction to the information in Figure 1?

ELM BAPTIST CHURCH

Sun Sch 9:30 AM-Wor 11 AM & 6 PM
Senior Adults-Wed 10:30 AM-7 PM
Bible Study-Childrens Clubs-Youth
Spanish Speaking Services Available
Rev John Miller-Sr. Pastor
Richard Lee-Assistant Pastor

N 46th & Sunnyside..................................491-4354

GOLDEN CARE PLUS
Associated With City Hospital
1550 N 115th 365-7587
Green Senior Center 525 N 85th..............447-7841
Hamption House For Senior Citizens
5225 15th NE...524-0473
Hanley Nutrition Site 1210 SW 136th......448-5768
Hanley Senior Center 1210 SW 136th.......244-3686
HOME REPAIRS FOR THE ELDERLY
500 30th St...447-7802
HOMESHARING FOR SENIORS
1601 2nd Ave Suite 800.........................448-5725
Independent Living 1715 E Cherry..........322-3637
Indochina/Chinese Elderly Association
409 Maynard St.......................................624-9577
June Valley Senior Center
105 2nd Ave NE.....................................392-2381
LA EASEL RESTAURANT
2524 16th 329-3837
Lifetime Learning Center 202 John..........283-5523
Lifetime Services Inc
800 5th Ave Suite 800............................622-8220
MEALS-ON-WHEELS
1601 2nd Ave Suite 800.........................448-5767
North Senior Center
9929 NE 180th 8th................................487-2441
Northwest Senior Center 4429 32 NW......447-7811
Norton Day Care For Adults
9250 14th NW...784-8285
Nutrition Projects for Senior Citizens
1601 2d Suite 800..................................448-5768
Pederson John Social Services
3015 37th SW..935-3020
Red Cross Aid To Aging
1900 25th Av S..323-2345
Senior Center of Weston
4217 SW Oregon......................................932-4044

SENIOR MEAL PROGRAM
1601 2nd Ave Suite 800.........................448-5768
SENIOR INFORMATION & ASSISTANCE
1601 2nd Ave Suite 800.........................448-3110
SENIOR REFERRAL SERVICE............344-5767
Senior Rights Assistance
1601 2nd Ave Suite 800.........................448-5720
SENIOR RIGHTS ASSISTANCE
1601 2nd Ave Suite 800........................ 448-5720
Senior Services
211 Burnett N...235-2533
SENIOR SERVICES OF SEATTLE/KING COUNTY
1601 2nd Ave Suite 800.........................448-5757
Central Area
500-30th Ave S.....................................447-7816
Greenwood
525 N 85th St...447-7841
First Hill
800 Jefferson St....................................448-5748
Southeast Seattle
7315-39th Ave S...................................722-0317
Northwest
5429-32nd Ave NW................................447-7811
Tallmadge Hamilton House
5225-15th Ave NE.................................524-0473
Wallingford
4649 Sunnyside Ave N..........................447-7825
West Seattle
4217 SW Oregon St..............................932-4044
Black Diamond
6th & Lawson.......................................886-2418
Maple Valley
22010 SE 248th....................................432-3222
Bothell
9929 NE 180th.......................................487-2441
Shoreline
835 NE 155th...365-1536
Sno-Valley
Stossel & Commercial Sts....................333-4152
Vashon-Maury
SW 176th St...463-5173
Share The Ride Club P O Box 80325........246-7881
Shoreline Senior Adult Multi Service Center
835 NE 155th...365-1536
Southeast Seattle Senior Center
4655 S Holly St.....................................722-0317
SPECIALIZED TRANSPORTATION
1601 2nd Ave Suite 800.........................448-5740
Wallingford Senior Center
4649 Sunnyside N.................................447-7825
White Center Nutrition Program
9002 16th SW...762-8762

Figure 1

chapter 8

Equality for All?

A First Look

A. Background Building

DIRECTIONS: Look at the illustration on the preceding page and answer the following questions.

1. What is happening in the illustration?

2. What does the man with the stop sign think?

3. How does the black woman feel?

4. This woman is a member of a minority group because she is black. What are some other minority groups in the United States?

5. What does *opportunity for all* mean?

6. The following is a quote from the Civil Rights Act of 1964:

   "No person in the United States shall, on the ground of race, color or national origin, be excluded from participation in . . . any program receiving federal financial assistance."

   Explain what this quote means in your own words.

B. Topic

DIRECTIONS: Before you begin to read, look at these topics. There is one topic for each paragraph. Look quickly at the reading to find these topics. Do not read every word at this point. Write the number of the paragraph next to the topic of that paragraph.

1. _____ American society

2. _____ more about discrimination

3. _____ equal opportunity laws

4. _____ questions about possibilities for minorities

5. _____ definitions of prejudice and discrimination

6. _____ examples of self-made men

C. Reading

DIRECTIONS: Now read.

1   Can a poor country boy from the hills of Kentucky become President of the United States? Can a poor, black, city boy become wealthy and famous all over the world? Can a woman become President of the United States? The answer to all of these questions is "yes, ideally it is possible." The key word here is "ideally." Ideally, everyone in the United States, whether rich or poor, has an equal opportunity to succeed.

2   This concept of equal opportunity to succeed is a basic idea in capitalism, the economic system of the United States. Social classes or levels are not permanently established. The terms *upper class* or *upper-middle class* are mainly financial terms, although an upper-class person has been wealthy for a long time. There are no kings, queens, or other royalty in the United States, and a person's background is not as important as that person's position now. Perhaps because the United States is a country of immigrants, people who often had very little when they arrived in the country, Americans value the ability to go "from rags to riches."

3   The first two examples in the first paragraph are descriptions of self-made men, who started life with almost nothing and became successful. These men are President Abraham Lincoln and the boxer Mohammed Ali. These two men did not have the advantages of wealth, good educational opportunities, or contact with powerful people. However, they were ambitious and wanted to succeed.

4   Of course, it is unrealistic to say that everyone who wants to succeed will be able to succeed. But there are laws which give every person in the United States the chance or opportunity to succeed. These laws guarantee equal opportunities for education and employment to all people. These laws are especially important to members of minorities (i.e., any group of people not white, Protestant, and male in the United States) such as Hispanics, women, blacks, and many other ethnic, religious, and racial groups. Minority groups may find that they do not have equal education, housing, or employment. They may have difficulty finding jobs or getting adequate pay because of prejudice.

5   Prejudice is a negative feeling against a person because of his or her race, religion, or background. For example, if a factory owner does not like Mexican-Americans in general, this person is prejudiced. A prejudiced person actually prejudges a whole group of people and feels negatively about all the people in that group. If a factory owner feels prejudiced, this is not a problem. The problem arises when this factory owner refuses to hire someone because of prejudice. If an employer gives a job to a man instead of a woman

1
2
3
4
5
6
7
8
9
10
11
12
13
14
15
16
17
18
19
20
21
22
23
24
25
26
27
28
29
30
31
32
33
34
35
36
37
38
39
40
41
42

when both are equally qualified, this is called discrimination. Dis-   43
crimination in housing, education, and employment is illegal in this   44
country.   45

6   The word *discrimination* really means the observation of dif-   46
ferences. Obviously, there are differences in people. However, equal   47
opportunity laws try to prevent differences from becoming prob-   48
lems when people want to succeed. In education, employment, and   49
many other areas, discrimination is a bad word.   50

React

Underline one sentence which you found interesting in
the reading. Read it to a partner.

D. Scanning/Vocabulary

Part 1

DIRECTIONS: Scan the reading for these words. Write the number of the line where you
find them. Then compare the meaning in the sentence to the meaning of the
word(s) on the right. Are the words similar or different? Write similar or different on the line.

	LINE NUMBER		SIMILAR OR DIFFERENT
1. country	_____	city	_____
2. key	_____	important	_____
3. ideally	_____	really	_____
4. equal	_____	same	_____
5. capitalism	_____	economic system	_____
6. background	_____	experience	_____
7. rags	_____	riches	_____
8. guarantee	_____	promise	_____
9. prejudice	_____	feeling	_____
10. prevent	_____	stop	_____

Part 2

DIRECTIONS: Find a word in the reading which has a meaning similar to the
following. The line number is given.

1. chance (7)   _____

2. do well (7)   _____

3. classes (9) _____

4. fixed (10) _____

5. benefit (21) _____

6. determined (23) _____

7. enough (34) _____

8. give a job (41) _____

9. able (43) _____

10. against the law (44) _____

E. Reading Comprehension

DIRECTIONS: Circle the letter of the choice that best completes each sentence.

1. According to the author, a woman _____ become President of the United States.

   a. can never   b. can ideally   c. probably will not

2. Abraham Lincoln and Mohammed Ali were born _____.

   a. rich   b. black   c. poor

3. Lincoln and Ali succeeded _____ wealth, good educational opportunities, and powerful friends.

   a. because of   b. in order to get   c. without

4. Generally speaking, social classes in the United States are _____.

   a. permanently   b. royalty   c. financial
      established   divisions

5. It is _____ to refuse to give someone a job because of race, religion, or sex.

   a. intelligent   b. illegal   c. guaranteed

6. Americans value the concept of equal opportunity because _____.

   a. many Americans   b. Americans like   c. many poor
      are wealthy   money   immigrants
                                                    became rich

7. There _____ laws which guarantee equal opportunity.

   a. are no   b. should be   c. are

8. _____ is illegal.

   a. Discrimination   b. A minority   c. Prejudice

9. Discrimination is a problem because it does not give people ——.

   a. the same chance   b. an easy life   c. prejudice
      to succeed

10. The author thinks that ——.

   a. there is equality in   b. prejudice is illegal   c. discrimination is a
      the United States   serious problem

Look Again

A. Vocabulary

DIRECTIONS: Circle the letter of the choice that best completes each sentence.

1. Laws can _____ discrimination, but not prejudice.

   a. succeed   b. prevent   c. guarantee

2. A famous person is a person _____ knows.

   a. everybody   b. somebody   c. nobody

3. A king and queen are members of _____.

   a. immigrants   b. royalty   c. employment

4. _____ is not a member of a minority in the United States.

   a. A black Puerto Rican   b. A white male   c. A female

5. The food was adequate. Everyone had _____ to eat.

   a. a lot   b. very little   c. the right amount

6. A person who is prejudiced against Hispanics has a(n) _____ feeling about them.

   a. negative   b. beneficial   c. advantageous

7. I want a job. Will you _____ me in your company?

   a. provide   b. succeed   c. hire

8. She refused. Her answer was _____.

   a. positive   b. negative   c. prejudice

9. I bought the house because I plan to live here _____.

   a. permanently   b. negatively   c. unrealistically

10. Discrimination in housing means that a landlord does not rent because _____.

    a. there is no apartment available   b. the people are unpleasant   c. of prejudice

B. Reading Comprehension

DIRECTIONS: Complete the following.

1. In paragraph 1, the author gives three examples of opportunities to succeed. What are they?

   1. _____

   2. _____

   3. _____

2. In paragraph 2, the author explains the concept of equal opportunity in the United States with two ideas. What are they?

3. What are the names of the two men given as examples in paragraph 1?

4. In what areas do minorities find prejudice?

5. Give one example of prejudice and one of discrimination. Remember discrimination is an action; prejudice is a feeling.

C. Think About It

1. When Irish immigrants first came to Boston, they sometimes read job notices that said "No Irish need apply." Many subsequent groups experienced discrimination. Is there discrimination in your country against immigrants?

2. Why do you think that people discriminate? Why are they prejudiced?

D. Survey Reading

There are laws in the United States to protect people from discrimination and to help them to succeed. In the 1950s, success was a house in the suburbs. Look at Figure 1 and answer the questions which follow.

1. What is the most important element of success for Americans according to this survey?

2. According to the survey, do Americans want to be rich and famous?

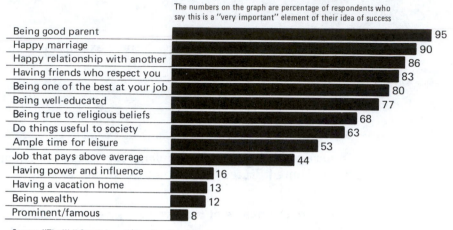

Very Important Elements of Success in America

The numbers on the graph are percentage of respondents who say this is a "very important" element of their idea of success

Being good parent	95
Happy marriage	90
Happy relationship with another	86
Having friends who respect you	83
Being one of the best at your job	80
Being well-educated	77
Being true to religious beliefs	68
Do things useful to society	63
Ample time for leisure	53
Job that pays above average	44
Having power and influence	16
Having a vacation home	13
Being wealthy	12
Prominent/famous	8

Source: "The Wall Street Journal/American Dream" survey conducted by The Roper Organization, February 1987

Figure 1

3. Does this survey show that friendship is important to Americans?

4. Which is more important to Americans according to this survey: good jobs, families, friends, or education? Put these in order of importance.

Contact a Point of View

A. Background Building

Look at the picture. Who are the two people? What does the man mean by pointing his finger toward the door? In the United States when can you ask an employee to leave his or her job? How about in your country?

B. Timed Reading

DIRECTIONS: *Read the following point of view and answer the questions in four minutes.*

Silvia Garcia, a black woman, applied for a job at a small company. One question on the application form was "Who else lives at your home address?" Ms. Garcia did not answer this question. She left the space blank.

The owner of the company, Jeff Erler, was a very religious man. He had started the company himself and felt that his employees were like his extended family. Mr. Erler interviewed Ms. Garcia personally. He noticed that she had marked "single" on her application and he was surprised that she was not married at her age. When he mentioned this to her, she just laughed and did not comment. He decided that she was a very nice woman. He also needed to hire members of minorities, so he hired her.

Ms. Garcia did very well in the company. In a few months she got a raise and was happy with the additional money. However, seven months after Mr. Erler hired her, he overheard a conversation in the cafeteria. Two other workers were talking about her and "the guy she's living with."

Mr. Erler called Ms. Garcia into his office that afternoon. He questioned her about her living situation and she admitted that she was living with her boyfriend. Mr. Erler told her that he was very sorry, but he did not want immoral people to work in his company. At first, she could not believe that Mr. Erler was serious. She told him that he had no right to call her immoral because she was living with her boyfriend. She said that as long as she was a good worker, her personal life was her own business and that he could not make judgments about it. Mr. Erler fired Ms. Garcia.

DIRECTIONS: Read each of the following sentences carefully to determine whether each is true (T), false (F), or impossible to know (ITK).

1. _____ Ms. Garcia was a member of a minority group.

2. _____ When Ms. Garcia applied for the job, she lived with her boyfriend.

3. _____ Ms. Garcia was not a good worker.

4. _____ Mr. Erler was a religious man.

5. _____ All Mr. Erler's employees were religious.

6. _____ Ms. Garcia's boyfriend worked in the same company.

7. _____ No one at the company except Mr. Erler knew that Ms. Garcia was living with someone.

8. _____ Ms. Garcia told Mr. Erler that she was not living with her boyfriend.

9. _____ Ms. Garcia was thirty years old.

10. _____ Ms. Garcia lost her job at Mr. Erler's company.

C. Vocabulary

DIRECTIONS: Circle the letter of the word(s) with the same meaning as the italicized word(s).

1. Who *else* lives at this address?

   a. related   b. in addition   c. only

2. The page was *blank.*

   a. empty   b. written   c. full

3. Leave a *space* between the lines of our compositions.

   a. meaning   b. certain area   c. sentence

4. I *applied* for a loan at the bank.

   a. questioned   b. gave money   c. tried to get

5. A politician often says, "*No comment.*"

   a. I have nothing to say   b. I don't know   c. Don't talk to me

6. Our office *hired* someone just yesterday.

   a. fired   b. gave more money to   c. gave a job to

7. I spoke with the director *personally.*

   a. myself   b. quickly   c. immediately

8. Her *personal* life is very interesting.

   a. social   b. private   c. love

9. If he steals money from poor people, he is *immoral.*

   a. rich   b. arrested   c. without values

10. I need a *raise.* I cannot support myself with this salary.

    a. job   b. higher pay   c. vacation with
    for the same job   more money

D. React

DIRECTIONS: Reread the information about Silvia Garcia and Jeff Erler. Then answer the following questions and share your ideas with the class.

1. What do you think Ms. Garcia does next?

   _____ collects unemployment insurance?

   _____ looks for another job?

_____ goes to see a lawyer?

_____ _____?

2. Do you think that Mr. Erler was fair to Ms. Garcia?

3. Do you think that Mr. Erler did anything illegal when he fired her?

4. Did Mr. Erler discriminate against her because of:
   her race?
   her sex?
   her religion?
   her personal background?
   her moral values?

5. Do you think this is discrimination? Is it an unfair employment procedure?

Optional Activity

If you decide that this case is an example of discrimination or unfair employment procedures, take it to court. Act out the parts of these people:

Silvia Garcia
Steve Kennedy, Silvia's boyfriend
Jeff Erler
Alice Lee, Jeff's secretary
The lawyers who help Silvia Garcia
The lawyers who help Jeff Erler
A judge, who also organizes the trial
A jury of people who decide the final judgment

Step 1: Meet in groups to decide what roles and positions you will take.
Step 2: Meet in court and present the evidence.
Step 3: Wait for the jury's decision.

E. Word Analysis

Part 1

DIRECTIONS: Look at the endings below for nouns and verbs. Are the italicized words in the sentences <u>nouns</u> or <u>verbs</u>?

NOUNS	VERBS
produc*tion*	produce
adjust*ment*	adjust
real*ity*	real*ize*

	NOUN	VERB

1. I'll help you *familiarize* yourself with the city.

2. *Discrimination* in hiring is illegal.

3. How did you *solve* that problem?

4. Could you *repeat* that please?

5. I made an *adjustment* in the plan.

6. I don't have a *solution* to that problem.

7. His *identity* is still a question.

8. What is your *community* like?

9. We can't *produce* that many machines.

10. Can you *identify* the problem?

Part 2

1. Study the meanings of these: Another example:

judi-	judge	**preju**dice	_____
pre-	before	**pre**register	_____
post-	after	**post**pone	_____
equ-	equal	ade**qu**ate	_____
leg-	law	**leg**islature	_____

2. Complete the sentences with one of the above words.

   a. They never finished the project because the money the government gave for the project wasn't _____.

   b. The _____ made a decision when they met last month.

   c. If you don't _____ for next semester, you will have to wait in long lines when classes start.

   d. The landlord wouldn't let her rent the apartment when he found out she was a student. She felt that this was _____.

   e. I hate to do my homework, so I usually _____ it for as long as possible.

3. Write the meaning of the boldfaced word on the line.

a. There are some **inequities** in the new tax law, but I'm sure the government will work them out eventually. _____

b. The **judge** hasn't made a decision yet in the case. _____

c. I got a ticket for parking in an **illegal** space. _____

d. I can't **prevent** you from going there, but I think you're making a mistake.

_____

e. I'd like to do **postgraduate** work in biochemistry. _____

Look Back

A. Vocabulary

DIRECTIONS: Circle the letter of the choice that best completes each sentence.

1. The _____ man did not like his daughter's boyfriend because he was Chinese.

   a. prejudiced   b. advantageous   c. adequate

2. I don't know if this color is green or gray. I don't have very good color _____.

   a. prejudice   b. discrimination   c. equality

3. There were two men and twelve women in the class. The men were in the _____.

   a. minority   b. percentage   c. opportunity

4. I found a job easily because my father _____ me to work for him.

   a. hired   b. gave   c. refused

5. I decided to quit before the owner _____ me.

   a. raised   b. fired   c. felt

6. With a degree in business, she was highly _____ to work in the company.

   a. qualified   b. adequate   c. prejudiced

7. There is a six-month _____ on this radio. If it breaks in that time, you can get another one for free.

   a. age   b. guarantee   c. qualification

8. I _____ a raise. I don't know if I will get one or not.

   a. prevented   b. fired   c. applied for

9. I can't _____ him. He doesn't answer his phone.

   a. adjust to   b. contact   c. give

10. I am very _____. I want to succeed and be at the top of my profession.

    a. ambitious   b. economic   c. self-made

B. Matching

DIRECTIONS: Find the word or phrase in column B which has a similar mean-ing to a word in column A. Write the letter of that word or phrase next to the word in column A.

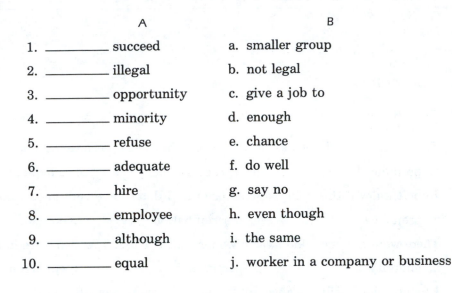

	A		B
1.	_____ succeed	a.	smaller group
2.	_____ illegal	b.	not legal
3.	_____ opportunity	c.	give a job to
4.	_____ minority	d.	enough
5.	_____ refuse	e.	chance
6.	_____ adequate	f.	do well
7.	_____ hire	g.	say no
8.	_____ employee	h.	even though
9.	_____ although	i.	the same
10.	_____ equal	j.	worker in a company or business

C. Synthesis Questions

1. Choose a famous person. Go to the library and find some information about that person in the encyclopedia or other books.

2. What does success mean to you? Number the following in order of importance for you. Put "1" next to the most important and "2" next to the second most important and so forth.
   For me, success means having. . . .

   _____ a lot of money

   _____ a good job

   _____ friends

   _____ a husband or wife

   _____ children

   _____ a home

   _____ a car

D. Vocabulary Preview

DIRECTIONS: Circle all the words you can find below. Most of the words are from Chapter 9.

unjustpotmnesacaientreqppitdiscriminationmfeirnprejudiceseparatelecaqillegalwomi
nqualifiedseriousgamitovblacksmubvetumidanpersistbinocitaminminorityduncacola
mprotectionheritagenolitdisadvantageinequalityraminracialslavestinomparticipation

Racial Issues

A First Look

A. Background Building

Racial issues are very deep and complex. Think about your own experience with people from races different from your own by answering this survey.

About your childhood. . . . Circle the answer.

1. When I was a child, I lived in a neighborhood that was racially _____.
   a. mixed   b. segregated.

2. My childhood friends were from _____.
   a. my race   b. other races.

3. My school was racially _____.
   a. mixed   b. segregated.

4. As a child, I _____ saw people who were from a different race.
   a. often   b. sometimes   c. almost never

About now. . . .

1. The neighborhood I live in today is racially _____.
   a. mixed   b. segregated.

2. I have friends _____.
   a. from many different races   b. mainly from my race   c. only from my race.

B. Topic

DIRECTIONS: Before you begin to read, look at these topics. There is one topic for each paragraph. Look quickly at the reading to find these topics. Do not read every word at this point. Write the number of the paragraph next to the topic of that paragraph.

1. _____ prejudice in the South

2. _____ prejudice and discrimination are problems in the United States

3. _____ equal education

4. _____ time is the answer

5. _____ discrimination in the North

6. _____ equal employment

7. _____ blacks compared to other groups

C. Reading

DIRECTIONS: Now read.

1	Ironically, in the United States—a country of immigrants—prejudice and discrimination continue to be serious problems. There was often tension between each established group of immigrants and each succeeding group. As each group became more financially successful and more powerful, they excluded newcomers from full participation in the society. Prejudice and discrimination are part of our history; however, this prejudicial treatment of different groups is nowhere more unjust than with black Americans.

Ironically, in the United States—a country of immigrants— `1`
prejudice and discrimination continue to be serious problems. There `2`
was often tension between each established group of immigrants `3`
and each succeeding group. As each group became more financially `4`
successful and more powerful, they excluded newcomers from full `5`
participation in the society. Prejudice and discrimination are part `6`
of our history; however, this prejudicial treatment of different `7`
groups is nowhere more unjust than with black Americans. `8`

Blacks had distinct disadvantages. For the most part, they `9`
came to the "land of opportunity" as slaves and they were not free `10`
to keep their heritage and cultural traditions. Unlike most Euro- `11`
pean immigrants, blacks did not have the protection of a support `12`
group; sometimes slave owners separated members of the same `13`
family. They could not mix easily with the established society either `14`
because of their skin color. It was difficult for them to adapt to the `15`
American culture. Even after they became free people, they still `16`
experienced discrimination in employment, housing, education, and `17`
even in public facilities, such as restrooms. `18`

Until the twentieth century (1900s), the majority of the black `19`
population lived in the southern part of the United States. Then `20`
there was a population shift to the large cities in the North. Prej- `21`
udice against blacks is often associated with the South. Slavery was `22`
more common there and discrimination was usually more blatant `23`
(easier to see): Water fountains, restrooms, and restaurants were `24`
often designated "white only." `25`

In the North, discrimination was usually less obvious, but cer- `26`
tainly it created poor black neighborhoods, ghettos, in most large `27`
cities. This happened because of discrimination in housing and the `28`
movement of white city residents to the suburbs, often called "white `29`
flight." `30`

In the 1950s and 1960s, blacks fought to gain fair treatment, `31`
and they now have legal protection in housing, education, and em- `32`

ployment. Because their neighborhoods are segregated, many blacks   *33*
feel that educational opportunities are not adequate for their chil-   *34*
dren. Busing children from one neighborhood to another is one so-   *35*
lution to inequality in education. Naturally, all parents want the   *36*
best possible education for their children.   *37*

One attempt to equalize employment and educational oppor-   *38*
tunities for blacks and other minorities is "affirmative action." Af-   *39*
firmative action means that those in charge of businesses, organi-   *40*
zations, and institutions should take affirmative (positive) action to *41*
find minorities to fill jobs. Many whites are angry about this reg-   *42*
ulation, because very qualified people sometimes do not get jobs   *43*
when they are filled by people from a certain minority. People call   *44*
this practice "reverse discrimination."   *45*

The situation of blacks is better today than it was in the 1950s,   *46*
but racial tension persists. Time will be the real solution to the prob- *47*
lem of race.   *48*

5

6

7

React

Look at line 10. The author says that blacks came to the "land of opportunity" as slaves. Why are the words "land of opportunity" in quotes?

D. Scanning/Vocabulary

Part 1

DIRECTIONS: *Write the line number where you find the word(s). Then choose the best meaning for the word as it is used in that sentence.*

1. ironically   line number _____

   a. strangely   b. naturally   c. obviously

2. succeeding   line number _____

   a. coming before   b. successful   c. following

3. excluded   line number _____

   a. prevented   b. prejudiced   c. adjusted

4. heritage   line number _____

   a. property   b. cultural past   c. work

5. protection   line number _____

  a. conflict   b. involvement   c. safety

6. majority   line number _____

  a. a large number b. some   c. most

7. associated with line number _____

  a. compared to   b. connected with c. qualified for

8. attempt   line number _____

  a. gain   b. guarantee   c. effort

9. qualified   line number _____

  a. capable   b. hired   c. ambitious

10. reverse   line number _____

  a. opposite   b. done again   c. prevented

Part 2

DIRECTIONS: *Find a word that is the opposite of the one given. The line is given.*

1. line 3 new   _____
2. line 8 fair   _____
3. line 9 benefits   _____
4. line 10 free people   _____
5. line 13 mixed   _____
6. line 23 hidden   _____
7. line 32 unlawful   _____
8. line 33 mixed by race   _____
9. line 36 fairness   _____
10. line 43 inexperienced _____

E. Reading Comprehension

DIRECTIONS: *Circle the letter of the choice that best completes each sentence.*

1. Because of _____, blacks could not easily mix in American society.

  a. skin color   b. language   c. heritage

2. Special restrooms and water fountains for blacks were more common in _____.

   a. the North b. ghettos c. the South

3. _____ is one attempt to equalize education.

   a. Reverse discrimination b. White flight c. Busing

4. Blacks were different from other groups because they _____.

   a. came with the b. adapted easily c. did not have
   first settlers support groups

5. There _____ discrimination in the North.

   a. was b. wasn't c. was no

6. According to the author, there will be a solution to racial problems _____.

   a. in the future b. very soon c. because of the 1950s

7. Affirmative action is *most* beneficial for _____.

   a. minorities b. business c. qualified people

8. In the North, discrimination was _____ to see.

   a. easier b. more difficult c. less difficult

9. The author thinks that prejudice and discrimination _____ in the United States.

   a. are natural b. are the same for c. form part of
   all groups history

10. The author thinks that prejudice is ironic here because the United States is a country of _____.

   a. wealth b. immigrants c. established groups

Look Again

A. Vocabulary

DIRECTIONS: Circle the letter of the choice that best completes each sentence.

1. I love to eat; _____, I hate to cook.
   - a. ironically
   - b. naturally
   - c. financially

2. One _____ of city living is the high cost.
   - a. advantage
   - b. benefit
   - c. disadvantage

3. He was _____ from the club because of his religious beliefs.
   - a. participated
   - b. excluded
   - c. designated

4. Whites in the United States are the _____.
   - a. minority
   - b. majority
   - c. newcomers

5. The cruel _____ of slaves in the United States is difficult to believe.
   - a. treatment
   - b. protection
   - c. heritage

6. Although she didn't like him, he _____ in calling her.
   - a. associated
   - b. persisted
   - c. designated

7. Busing is a(n) _____ to equalize educational opportunities.
   - a. loss
   - b. attempt
   - c. participation

8. _____ public schools are not legal.
   - a. Integrated
   - b. Associated
   - c. Segregated

9. He is _____ to teach economics.
   - a. adequate
   - b. qualified
   - c. obvious

10. _____ discrimination is clear and easy to see.
    - a. Reverse
    - b. Blatant
    - c. Unjust

B. Reading Comprehension

1. Compare blacks to other groups who came to the U.S. Give two examples of disadvantages which they had.

2. Give two examples of discrimination against blacks.

3. Reread the information about equality in education and try to explain what busing means.

4. Affirmative action means that organizations try to fill jobs with minorities. Why do you think people should do this?

C. Think About It

1. Is there discrimination in your country? Is it racial? Social? Or sexual? What kind of discrimination takes place? Employment? Housing? Education?

D. Reading

DIRECTIONS: Study the following graph and answer the questions below.

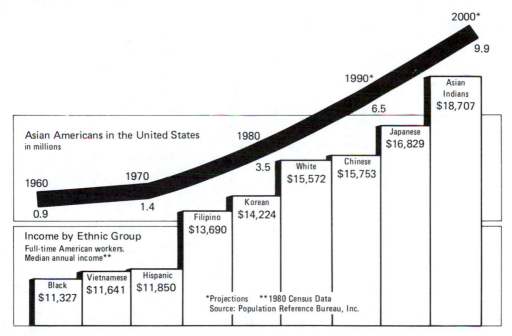

Source: Blumrich, *Newsweek*, May 11, 1987, p. 49.

The two graphs shown above are from an article about Asian Americans.

1. a. What does the "Asian Americans in the United States" graph measure?

   _____

   b. For how many years? _____

2. a. What does "Income by Ethnic Group" measure?

   _____

   b. Which ethnic group earns the most? _____

   c. Which ethnic group earns the least? _____

   d. What is the dollar difference between the highest earning Asian group and the lowest earning Asian group? _____

   e. How do Hispanics compare to the other ethnic groups? _____

   _____

   f. What reasons can you think of to explain the differences in income?

Contact a Point of View

A. Background Building

The affirmative action policies are difficult to understand. These policies suggest each organization should reflect the total population. For example, blacks make up about 15 percent of the population in the United States. If you own a small company with 100 employees, how many should be black?

B. Timed Reading

In the early 1970s, Allen Bakke, an engineer from California, decided that he wanted to change his career and become a doctor. He applied to the medical school at the University of California. Bakke was a

155

good student; he had graduated from the University of Minnesota with an A average and had a master's degree from Stanford. He was not accepted by the University of California. He was very upset.

Bakke discovered that the university had an affirmative action policy; he believed that some black students who were accepted to the medical school were not as qualified as he was. In other words, he felt that they were accepted because of their race and not because of their background. It seems that the university was trying to equalize educational opportunities for minority students. The university hoped that by accepting a certain number of minority students, they could change a long history of discrimination.

Bakke felt that this affirmative action policy was unjust and that he had a right to attend medical school. He felt that he was better qualified and that the action of the medical school was reverse discrimination. He considered the action illegal and decided to bring his problem to the court for a decision.

He brought the issue to two state courts in California. The decision of the judges was that the action of the medical school was perfectly legal and that Bakke had to accept this decision.

He then decided to bring the problem to the United States Supreme Court, where the final decision-making power in the United States lies. What do you think happened?

DIRECTIONS: Read each of the following statements carefully to determine whether each is true (T), false (F), or impossible to know (ITK).

1. _____ Bakke's background was better than most others.

2. _____ Bakke had a good background.

3. _____ Bakke applied to Stanford Medical School.

4. _____ This case happened last year.

5. _____ Reverse discrimination means not accepting minorities.

6. _____ The Supreme Court makes final decisions about laws in the United States.

7. _____ Bakke had no alternative after the decision of the two lower (state) courts.

8. _____ The policy of the school was to fill all places with minority students.

9. _____ The two state courts said that the action was illegal.

10. _____ Bakke accepted the decision of the state courts.

C. Vocabulary

DIRECTIONS: Fill in the blanks with vocabulary from the reading.

1. applied/accepted/attended

   Allen Bakke _____ the University of Minnesota as an under-

   graduate. He _____ to the University of California, but was

   not _____.

2. discrimination/judge/illegal

   The _____ considered that _____ in any

   form was _____.

3. applicants/accepted/backgrounds

   _____ who had _____ that were not as

   good as Bakke's were _____.

4. policy/attempt

   This _____ was an _____ to equalize op-

   portunities.

D. React

DIRECTIONS: Mr. Bakke's affirmative action case is a difficult one. According to the facts, what would you decide?
Get into groups of five and decide the case as the Supreme Court did. Remember that you must have a majority decision (3 to 2). After reaching your decision, present it to the class. Here is some useful vocabulary.

We feel that . . .

We agree that . . .

Mr. Bakke should . . .   legal/illegal

The university should . . .   necessary/unnecessary

All applicants should . . .   unconstitutional

Minority applicants must . . .

Racial discrimination . . .

Reverse discrimination . . .

E. Word Analysis

Part 1

DIRECTIONS: *Choose the appropriate word form for each sentence. Is it a noun or a verb?*

1. employ
   employment

2. Discriminate
   Discrimination

3. treat
   treatment

4. educate
   education

5. protect
   protection

6. equalize
   equality

7. associate
   association

8. designate
   designation

9. act
   action

10. solve
    solution

1. She is looking for _____.

2. _____ is unfortunately part of the history of this country.

3. What is the best way to _____ a cold?

4. Public schools should _____ everybody.

5. Don't worry. I'll _____ you.

6. Is the basis of democracy _____?

7. She denies any _____ with him.

8. The _____ of "white only" facilities is now over.

9. They always _____ natural.

10. Time isn't going to _____ this problem.

Part 2

DIRECTIONS: *In other chapters, you have studied parts of the **boldfaced** words in the following sentences. Write the letter with the correct meaning of the boldfaced word from the list below the sentences.*

1. They asked the government to **intervene** because the two groups couldn't come to any agreement. _____

2. He walked right past me as if I were **invisible**. _____

3. All I want is an **equitable** solution to the problem. _____

4. I'm going to **preview** the movie I'm planning to show in class tomorrow. _____

_____

5. I read that woman's **autobiography**. It was quite interesting. _____

   _____

6. Where's the **exit** to this building? _____

7. In my **judgment**, the driver was wrong. _____

8. I think he needs **psychiatric** help. _____

9. His leg was **visible** sticking out from behind the sofa. _____

10. Exercise has **beneficial** effects on your body and mind. _____

a. look at before
b. opinion
c. fair
d. story about your own life
e. mental

f. able to be seen
g. come between
h. way out
i. not able to be seen
j. good, positive

Look Back

A. Vocabulary

DIRECTIONS: Circle the letter of the choice that best completes each sentence.

1. The woman did not want the magazines, but the salesman was _____.

   a. exclusive　　　　b. protective　　　　c. persistent

2. This paper from the state court is filled with _____.

   a. tension　　　　b. legalities　　　　c. loss

3. She has everything in order: She _____ her work very carefully.

   a. segregates　　　　b. organizes　　　　c. associates

4. She makes all the important company decisions, all the _____ ones.

   a. reverse　　　　b. major　　　　c. minor

5. It is _____ to do that now. Don't wait.

   a. blatant　　　　b. advantageous　　　　c. succeeding

6. _____ speaking, I don't understand the situation at all.

   a. Unjustly　　　　b. Continuously　　　　c. Seriously

7. He _____ football with Americans.

   a. associates　　　　b. participates　　　　c. discriminates

8. Cats are very _____ of their kittens.

   a. protective　　　　b. serious　　　　c. affirmative

9. He has improved 100 percent. He has made great _____.

   a. attempts　　　　b. gains　　　　c. losses

10. He has very _____ taste; only the best for him.

    a. regulatory　　　　b. discriminating　　　　c. common

B. Matching

DIRECTIONS: *Find the word or phrase in column B which has a similar mean-ing to a word in column A. Write the letter of that word or phrase next to the word in column A.*

	A		B
1.	_____ naturally	a.	unfair
2.	_____ disadvantage	b.	positive
3.	_____ adequate	c.	tied with
4.	_____ legal	d.	different
5.	_____ participation	e.	enough
6.	_____ segregate	f.	easy to see
7.	_____ unjust	g.	obviously
8.	_____ qualified	h.	problem
9.	_____ associated	i.	lawful
10.	_____ blatant	j.	continue
11.	_____ serious	k.	able
12.	_____ majority	l.	important
13.	_____ distinct	m.	larger percentage
14.	_____ persist	n.	involvement
15.	_____ affirmative	o.	separate

C. Synthesis Questions

1. In the 1960s, the now famous case of Rosa Parks occurred; she was a black woman who would not give up her seat on the bus and move to the back. She was then arrested. Can that happen today?

2. In many places in the world, there are all male private clubs. How do you feel about all-male clubs? Find out if these are possible in the United States.

3. The Ku Klux Klan is an anti-black organization in this country. Its members are prejudiced against blacks. Why do you think this group exists? Is this group legal in the United States?

D. Look Ahead

What shorter words can you see in these words?

homemaker	(1) _____		generalize	(7) _____	
uncivilized	(2) _____		nontraditional	(8) _____	
alongside	(3) _____		essentially	(9) _____	
industrialized	(4) _____		residential	(10) _____	
postwar	(5) _____		dishwasher	(11) _____	
inventions	(6) _____		undeveloped	(12) _____	

chapter 10

The Role of Women in the United States

A First Look

A. Background Building

1. Complete these sentences about your country or culture.

   a. In the history of my country, women were _____.

       a. very active   b. fairly active   c. not active

   b. Forty years ago, a woman's life in my country was/was not different from a woman's life now because _____.

       For example, _____.

   c. Some typical jobs for women now are: _____

   _____.

   d. In the family, _____ takes care of the children.

       a. the mother   b. a relative   c. someone else

2. Look at the illustration on page 164. Where is she? What is happening? Why?

B. Topic

> DIRECTIONS: Write the topic of each paragraph in the reading. Do <u>not</u> write long sentences. Short phrases are fine.

    1. _____

    2. _____

    3. _____

    4. _____

    5. _____

    6. _____

C. Reading

DIRECTIONS: Now read.

American women experience a great variety of lifestyles. A
"typical" American woman may be single. She may also be di-
vorced or married. She may be a homemaker, a doctor, or a factory
worker. It is very difficult to generalize about American women.
However, one thing that many American women have in common
is their attitude about themselves and their role in American life.

Historically, American women have always been very independent. The first colonists to come to New England were often
young couples who had left behind their extended family (i.e., their
parents, sisters, cousins, etc.). The women were alone in a new, undeveloped country with their husbands. This had two important effects. First of all, this as yet uncivilized environment demanded that
every person share in developing it and in survival. Women worked
alongside their husbands and children to establish themselves in
this new land. Second, because they were in a new land without the
established influence of older members of society, women felt free
to step into nontraditional roles. In addition, there were no rules in
the Protestant religion which demanded that women stay in any
definite role.

This role of women was reinforced in later years as Americans
moved west, again leaving family behind and encountering a hostile
environment. Even later, in the East, as new immigrants arrived,
the women often found jobs more easily than men. Women became
the supporters of the family. The children of these early Americans
grew up with many examples of working women around them.

Within the established lifestyle of industrialized twentieth-
century America, the strong role of women was not as dramatic as
in the early days of the country. Some women were active outside
the home; others were not. However, when American men went to
war in the 1940s, women stepped into the men's jobs as factory and
business workers. After the war, some women stayed in these positions, and others left their jobs with a new sense of their own capabilities.

When men returned from the war and the postwar "baby
boom" began, Americans began to move in great numbers to the
suburbs. A new model of a traditional family developed, and women
were essentially separated from men. Men generally went back into
the city to work, and there was a strong division between work and
home. Houses in the suburbs were far apart from each other, and
these areas were all residential; there were no stores or businesses.
Women had to drive to buy food and to visit family and friends. All

1
2
3
4
5
6
7
8
9
10
11
12
13
14
15
16
17
18
19
20
21
22
23
24
25
26
27
28
29
30
31
32
33
34
35
36
37
38
39
40
41

these factors contributed to a sense of isolation and to a feeling of   42
separation between the family and the outside world. At the same   43
time technological developments gave American homemakers many   44
time-saving inventions such as dishwashers, vacuum cleaners, and   45
frozen foods. Life became easier for American homemakers but not   46
necessarily more satisfying. With more time on their hands, Amer-   47
ican women began to want to become more involved.   48

6   Many people think that the women's movement, a political and   49
social effort to give women the same status and rights as men, was   50
a result of this isolation and separation of women in the suburbs.   51
Given the historical model of women who were active outside the   52
home in building America, it is really not surprising that American   53
women are working to reestablish their strong role in American life.   54

React

Underline some information that surprised you in the reading. Share this with a classmate.

D. Scanning/Vocabulary

DIRECTIONS: Scan the reading for these words. Write the number of the line where you find them. Then compare its meaning in the sentence to the meaning of the word(s) on the right. Are the words similar or different? Write similar or different on the line.

	LINE NUMBER		SIMILAR OR DIFFERENT
1. lifestyle	_____	way of life	_____
2. divorced	_____	married	_____
3. attitude	_____	feeling	_____
4. couple	_____	two people	_____
5. uncivilized	_____	undeveloped	_____
6. share	_____	work together	_____
7. definite	_____	general	_____
8. reinforced	_____	strengthened	_____
9. hostile	_____	friendly	_____

10. positions   _____   jobs   _____

11. capabilities   _____   abilities   _____

12. division   _____   separation   _____

13. far apart   _____   close together   _____

14. contribute   _____   add   _____

15. satisfying   _____   boring   _____

E. Reading Comprehension

DIRECTIONS: Circle the letter of the choice that best completes each sentence.

1. The author thinks that there are _____ for American women.

   a. few possibilities   b. many choices   c. sometimes jobs

2. American women have felt independent _____.

   a. only recently   b. for several hundred years   c. since World War II

3. Traditions were _____ survival in this new land.

   a. as important as   b. less important than   c. only for

4. American women _____ west with their husbands.

   a. did not go   b. left   c. moved

5. In the early twentieth century, _____ American women worked.

   a. some   b. all   c. no

6. The move to the suburbs took place in the _____.

   a. 1700s   b. 1800s   c. 1900s

7. According to the author, life in the suburbs had a _____ effect on women.

   a. positive   b. negative   c. hostile

8. A _____ was absolutely necessary in the suburbs.

   a. business   b. car   c. baby boom

9. Technological developments gave women more _____.

   a. time   b. satisfaction   c. hands

10. The author feels that the women's movement has _____ a strong role for women.

   a. reestablished   b. worked for   c. worked against

Look Again

A. Vocabulary

DIRECTIONS: Circle the letter of the choice that best completes each sentence.

1. When there is little variety, people have _____.

   a. no time   b. few choices   c. a lot of diversity

2. The student had a negative attitude about her work. She _____.

   a. hated it   b. studied hard   c. tried a lot

3. A _____ is an example of a timesaver.

   a. watch   b. dishwasher   c. bed

4. There were no other people. The boy was _____.

   a. undeveloped   b. social   c. alone

5. The young people felt that they needed no help from anyone. They were very _____.

   a. influenced   b. independent   c. uncivilized

6. A residential area has _____.

   a. stores   b. houses   c. businesses

7. I _____ difficulties in language when I traveled to the Soviet Union.

   a. encountered   b. established   c. contributed to

8. The young people tried hard. They showed a lot of _____.

   a. effort   b. status   c. influence

9. I _____ ten dollars to the organization.

   a. reinforced   b. shared   c. contributed

10. We make the same salaries, but our _____ is not the same because you have the title of "director."

    a. status   b. sense   c. model

B. Reading Comprehension

DIRECTIONS: Complete this outline of the reading.

Paragraph 1

This paragraph states that (circle the answer):

a. all American women are similar

b. American women are hard to make generalizations about

Paragraph 2

Some reasons why women worked hard and stepped into nontraditional roles:

_____

_____

_____

Paragraph 3

Another reason why women had strong roles:

_____

Paragraph 4

In the twentieth century, _____

until _____ when _____

Paragraph 5

Some reasons why women wanted to get more involved:

_____

_____

_____

Paragraph 6

Conclusion: _____

_____

C. Think About It

1. Go back to the reading.

   a. Find two facts and underline them.

   b. Find one opinion. Underline it.

   c. Find out if your classmates agree about whether these are facts or opinions.

2. Read these paragraphs. Choose only one word or phrase from each box to give your opinion or information about your country or culture. Discuss your ideas with a classmate.

should—something is a good idea.   *I should get enough sleep.*
have to—something is necessary.   *I have to take an exam tomorrow.*
be supposed to—a law, rule, or agree-   *They are supposed to meet me here.*
ment   *We aren't supposed to smoke in this room.*

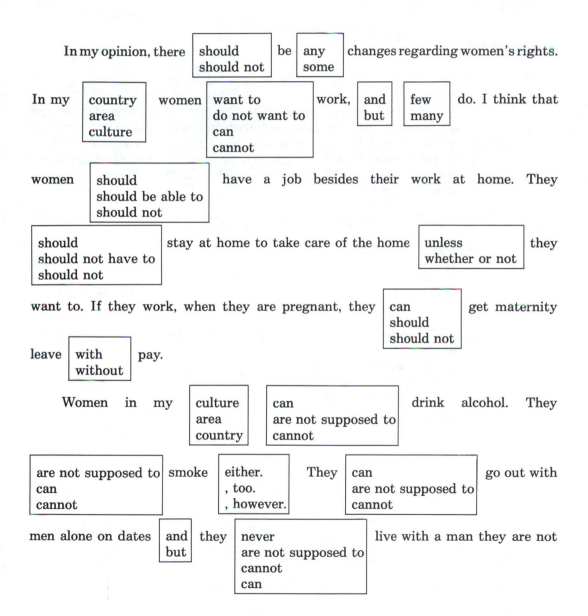

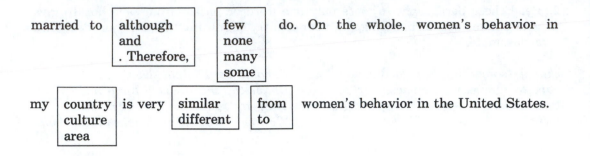

married to | although | | few | do. On the whole, women's behavior in
and | none
. Therefore, | many
some

my | country | is very | similar | from | women's behavior in the United States.
culture | different | to
area

D. Reading

DIRECTIONS: Read and answer the questions below.

Margaret Lee and Peter Erickson got married a couple of years ago. Margaret kept her own name and everyone continued to call her Margaret Lee except her mother-in-law. She introduces Margaret as Margaret Erickson and sends her letters addressed to "Mrs. Peter Erickson" instead of "Ms. Margaret Lee." Margaret and Peter have just named their first child Michael Lee-Erickson.

1. What are the problems in this situation?

2. Who is unhappy?

3. Is there any solution to these problems?

4. What is the system for women and children's last names in your country?

5. Some other language changes that resulted from the women's movement:
   housewife → homemaker
   girl, lady → woman
   Mrs., Miss → Ms.
   Why do you think women wanted these changes?

Contact a Point of View

A. Background Building

1. Write the names of the things the woman is carrying in the above illustration.

2. Why is she carrying them? What do these things show?

3. What do you think this reading will be about?

B. Timed Reading

DIRECTIONS: Read the following point of view and answer the questions in four minutes.

Jane Brown has been married for twelve years. She has three children and lives in a suburb outside Columbus, Ohio. When her youngest child reached school age, Jane decided to go back to work. She felt that she should contribute to the household finances; her salary could make the difference beween a financial struggle and a secure financial situation for her family. Jane also felt bored and frustrated in her role as a homemaker and wanted to be more involved in life outside her home.

Jane was worried about her children's adjustment to this new situation, but she arranged for them to go stay with a woman nearby after school each afternoon. They seem to be happy with the arrangement. The problems seem to be between Jane and her husband, Bill.

When Jane was at home all day, she was able to clean the house, go grocery shopping, wash the clothes, take care of the children, and cook two or three meals each day. She was very busy, of course, but she succeeded in getting everything done. Now these same things need to be done, but Jane has only evenings and early mornings to do them.

Both Jane and Bill are tired when they arrive home at 6:00 P.M. Bill is accustomed to sitting down and reading the paper or watching TV until dinner is ready. This is exactly what Jane feels like doing, but someone has to fix dinner and Bill expects it to be Jane. Jane is becoming very angry at Bill's attitude. She feels that they should share the household jobs; Bill feels that everything should be the same as it was before Jane went back to work.

DIRECTIONS: Read each of the following statements carefully to determine whether each is true (T), false (F), or impossible to know (ITK).

1. _____ Jane Brown lives in Columbus, Indiana.

2. _____ Money was one of the reasons why Jane wanted to work.

3. _____ Jane liked her life as a homemaker.

4. _____ Jane was married once before her marriage to Bill.

5. _____ Jane and Bill wake up at 6:00 A.M.

6. _____ Jane wants to relax now after work.

7. _____ Jane is a secretary.

8. _____ They were rich before Jane went back to work.

9. _____ Jane worked at some time before this.

10. _____ Jane and Bill work in the same building.

C. Vocabulary

DIRECTIONS: Circle the letter of the word(s) with the same meaning as the italicized word.

1. I can't *contribute* any time to your program, but I will be happy to help out with money.

   a. give   b. take   c. have

2. There was a *struggle* between the two children over the football.

   a. fight   b. value   c. plan

3. After they put the money in the bank, they were sure that it was *secure*.

   a. broken   b. safe   c. difficult

4. What an *adjustment* it is to move from Florida to Vermont in January!

   a. problem   b. exclusion   c. changing process

5. We were *tired* because we did not get very much sleep.

   a. exhausted   b. unhappy   c. forced

6. Her *salary* is very high in her new job.

   a. hours   b. status   c. pay

7. They are both very *active* in their school.

   a. different   b. involved   c. absent

8. They may change their plans because they are not happy with the *arrangement*.

   a. situation   b. problems   c. people

9. She was unhappy with her *role* as homemaker.

   a. time   b. position   c. house

10. What were the *effects* of the decision she made?

   a. results   b. reasons   c. causes

D. React

DIRECTIONS: *Read the timed reading again. Work with another student and answer the following questions. When you are finished, compare your ideas for numbers 5 and 6 with the other students' ideas.*

1. What are the problems for Jane Brown?

2. What are the problems for the children?

3. What are the problems for Bill?

4. What are Jane's responsibilities?

5. What are three (3) possible solutions for these problems?

6. What should Jane and Bill do?

E. Word Analysis

Part 1

DIRECTIONS: Choose the appropriate word form for each sentence. Is it a noun, adjective, or verb?

1. vary
   various
   variety

2. social
   socialize
   society

3. tradition
   traditional

4. industry
   industrial
   industrialize

5. reside
   residence
   residential

6. change
   changeable

7. religion
   religious

8. care
   careful

9. separate
   separable
   separation

10. secure
    security

1. There is little _____ in my job.

2. I can't believe that you hate to _____.

3. This program is quite _____.

4. Pittsburgh is an _____ city.

5. The census states that three people _____ at that address.

6. The weather here is _____.

7. She seems like a _____ person.

8. Take _____. You might fall.

9. I cannot _____ these two pages.

10. Financial _____ is important to some people.

Part 2

1. Study the meaning of these:

   Another example:

   dict - say   predict   _____

   resid - remain sitting
                    residential   _____

tech - design	technology	_____
fort - strong	reinforce	_____
- sta - firm	established	_____

2. Complete the sentences with one of the above words.

    a. Homework can _____ what I study in class.

    b. Computer _____ has developed significantly in the last ten years.

    c. You can never _____ the weather with 100 percent certainty.

    d. The first government _____ laws and procedures.

    e. Is this area of the city commercial or _____?

F. Skimming/Scanning

Female Executives and Their Families

How Are Home Responsibilities Handled?

Chores	Wife	Shared	Husband	Can't Say	Children	Wife	Shared	Husband	Can't Say
Paying the bills	54%	25%	21%	*	Shopping for their clothes	70%	17%	3%	10%
Seeing that the laundry is done	52	28	7	13	Managing their excursions and activities	37	46	5	12
Planning meals and shopping for food	47	41	8	4	Tending to them at home when they are ill	30	49	5	16
Planning investments	24	60	15	1	Disciplining them	13	73	4	10

*Less than one percent

Figure 1

DIRECTIONS: Answer the following questions about Figure 1.

1. Skim the chart. What does it show? _____

_____

2. Which chore do men and women share most often?

_____

3. Who usually pays the bills? _____

4. Which chores do men rarely have primary responsibility for?

_____

5. Which responsibility for children do women usually take responsibility for?

_____

6. Which responsibility for children do men and women share most often?

_____

7. Does this information represent the average American family?

_____

Look Back

A. Vocabulary

DIRECTIONS: Circle the letter of the choice that best completes each sentence.

1. The young man never questioned anything and did everything in the same way that his parents did. He was very _____.

    a. uncivilized   b. traditional   c. divorced

2. My _____ to the group was small, but they were happy to have help.

    a. contribution   b. establishment   c. solution

3. The _____ of cities in the West was important to early Americans.

    a. area   b. establishment   c. responsibility

4. An understanding of the past or a(n) _____ view is important for people today.

    a. ironic   b. Protestant   c. historical

5. The worker was good at his job and did it with _____.

    a. ease   b. factors   c. lifestyle

6. The army was losing the struggle against the enemy and needed _____, other groups of fighters and ammunition.

    a. society   b. exhaustion   c. reinforcements

7. She was very active in politics. Her _____ resulted in a government job.

    a. environment   b. involvement   c. advantage

8. The politician thanked her _____ for their help.

    a. supporters   b. factors   c. couples

9. I want to build a house, so I am looking for _____.

    a. land   b. environment   c. society

10. When should we go on our picnic? Time, weather, and hunger are the three _____ to think about.

    a. inventions   b. positions   c. factors

B. Matching

DIRECTIONS: Find the word or phrase in column B which has a similar mean-ing to a word in column A. Write the letter of that word or phrase next to the word in column A.

	A		B
1. _____	isolated	a.	job
2. _____	sense	b.	diversity
3. _____	active	c.	separated
4. _____	tired	d.	meet
5. _____	encounter	e.	exhausted
6. _____	position	f.	feeling
7. _____	variety	g.	involved
8. _____	secure	h.	only one
9. _____	alone	i.	safe
10. _____	arrange	j.	organize

C. Synthesis Questions

1. Has there been a women's movement in your country? Explain some-thing about women's roles in your country. Discuss work, home, and relationships between men and women.

2. If you were going to draw an illustration about the women's move-ment, what would you draw? Discuss your ideas with a classmate.

3. Interview a man or woman about some of the issues you discussed in number 1. Work with your classmates to develop your questions. Re-port what you find out to the class.

D. Vocabulary Preview

DIRECTIONS: Circle all the words you can find below. Most of the words are from Chapter 11.

```
eduemisusevspendtendtoconflictingincludetunirosubjectimk
salariedgkriemsalesmeitpercentagewriexciselqrstatejurats
tuezrevenuepuivehicleslbhrutilizenruerepairsirtaxorncgdr
wetypesbsfederalrtebcomplaineurnsiewdtaxesiogummunicipal
```

Taxes, Taxes, and More Taxes

A First Look

A. Background Building

Look at the picture on the preceding page. The man is giving money to someone. Who is the man taking the money? What does that man represent? The man is paying taxes. Why do people pay taxes?

Try answering these questions true or false before reading the article.

1. _____ In the United States, everyone pays taxes to the national government.

2. _____ All states charge taxes.

3. _____ The amount of money which you pay in taxes is 10% of your income.

4. _____ State tax laws are the same in every state.

5. _____ Americans have to pay taxes on their cars.

B. Topic

DIRECTIONS: Skim the reading. Write the topic of each paragraph on the following lines.

1. _____

2. _____

3. _____

4. _____

5. _____

6. _____

C. Reading

DIRECTIONS: Now read.

1   Americans often say that there are only two things a person can be sure of in life: death and taxes. Americans do not have a corner on the "death" market, but many people feel that the United States leads the world with the worst taxes.

2   Taxes consist of the money which people pay to support their government. There are generally three levels of government in the United States: federal, state, and city; therefore, there are three types of taxes.

3   Salaried people who earn more than four to five thousand dollars per year must pay a certain percentage of their salaries to the federal (national) government. The percentage varies for individuals. It depends on their salaries. The federal government has a two-level income tax; that is, 15 or 28 percent. $17,850 is the cutoff. The tax rate is 15 percent below $17,850 and 28 percent above. With the high cost of taxes, people are not very happy on April 15, when the federal taxes are due.

4   The second tax is for the state government: New York, California, North Dakota, or any of the other forty-seven states. Some states have an income tax similar to that of the federal government. Of course, the percentage for the state tax is lower. Other states have a sales tax, which is a percentage charged to any item which you buy in that state. For example, a person might want to buy a package of gum for twenty-five cents. If there is a sales tax of eight percent in that state, then the cost of the gum is twenty-seven cents. This figure includes the sales tax. Some states use income tax in addition to sales tax to raise their revenues. The state tax laws are diverse and confusing.

5   The third tax is for the city. This tax comes in two forms: property tax (residents who own a home have to pay taxes on it) and excise tax, which is levied on vehicles in a city. The cities utilize these funds for education, police and fire departments, public works (including street repairs, water and sanitation) and municipal buildings.

6   Since Americans pay such high taxes, they often feel that they are working one day each week just to pay their taxes. People always complain about taxes. They often protest that the government misuses their tax dollars. They say that it spends too much on useless and impractical programs. Although Americans have conflicting views on many issues—religious, racial, cultural, and political—they tend to agree on one subject: Taxes are too high.

React

Look at the reading again. Choose one sentence from it which surprised you. Write down the sentence and then explain to your classmates why it surprised you.

D. Scanning/Vocabulary

PART 1

DIRECTIONS: *Scan the reading for these words. Write the number of the line where you find them. Then compare its meaning in the sentence to the meaning of the word(s) on the right. Are the words similar or different? Write similar or different on the line.*

	LINE NUMBER		SIMILAR OR DIFFERENT
1. consist of	_____	are made of	_____
2. spend	_____	saves	_____
3. complain	_____	enjoy	_____
4. conflicting	_____	similar	_____
5. include	_____	keep out	_____
6. tend to	_____	seem to	_____
7. repairs	_____	rebuilding	_____
8. misuse	_____	use well	_____
9. subject	_____	opinion	_____
10. due	_____	payable	_____

PART 2

DIRECTIONS: *Find a word in the reading which has a meaning similar to the following. The line number is given.*

1. national (7) _____

2. kinds (8) _____

3. changes (11) _____

4. contains (25) _____

5. income (26) _____

6. city (32) _____

7. disagree strongly (36) _____

8. useless (38) _____

9. opinion (39) _____

10. problems (39) _____

E. Reading Comprehension

DIRECTIONS: Circle the letter of the choice that best completes each sentence.

1. In the United States, there are generally _____ basic types of taxes.

    a. two   b. three   c. four

2. A person must pay federal taxes if that person _____.

    a. has a part-time job   b. lives in certain states   c. earns more than a
                                                              few thousand
                                                              dollars

3. There are _____ basic types of city taxes.

    a. three   b. two   c. four

4. Some states tax items that a person buys. This is a(n) _____ tax.

    a. income   b. sales   c. excise

5. State sales taxes _____ in different states.

    a. are fixed   b. are based on income   c. vary greatly

6. Cities get tax money from two different sources: homeowners and _____.

    a. property   b. municipal employees   c. drivers

7. Americans think that they have to work one day out of every five to _____.

    a. pay the   b. relax   c. misuse their taxes
       government

8. Each of the _____ states probably has individual tax laws.

    a. forty-seven   b. three   c. fifty

9. If a person who earns $17,000 pays 15 percent of it in federal taxes, a person who earns $30,000 pays _____.

    a. 15 percent also   b. a lower percentage   c. more than $8,000

10. The author thinks that we can be certain about two things: _____.

    a. useless and   b. taxes and death   c. sales tax and
       impractical programs   income tax

Look Again

A. Vocabulary

DIRECTIONS: Circle the letter of the choice that best completes each sentence.

1. Taxes must be paid on a certain day. They are _____ on that day.

   a. sure   b. due   c. raised

2. A(n) _____ person earns an income.

   a. impractical   b. salaried   c. resident

3. The amount of income tax a person pays _____ his or her salary.

   a. depends on   b. earns   c. increases

4. People today are often careless, and we _____ our national resources.

   a. spend   b. complain about   c. misuse

5. You cannot agree. He has his _____ and you have yours.

   a. aspect   b. view   c. protest

6. The United States is a country of immigrants. There are many _____ of Americans.

   a. percentages   b. types   c. issues

7. When Americans don't like what the government is doing, they usually _____.

   a. include   b. protest   c. reinforce

8. When people from warm countries visit cold areas, they usually _____ about the weather.

   a. vary   b. complain   c. tend

9. It is _____ for a person who doesn't drive to buy a car.

   a. conflicting   b. impractical   c. confusing

10. Energy is one of the most important _____ of this century.

    a. issues   b. views   c. solutions

B. Reading Comprehension

DIRECTIONS: Fill out the information in the outline.

1. Americans can be sure of two things in life: _____

   and _____.

2. There are generally three types of taxes.

   a. _____

   b. _____

   c. _____

3. Income taxes vary for individuals.

   a. Those who earn less _____.

   b. Those who earn more _____.

4. Many individual states also charge taxes. Some have _____

   and others have _____.

5. City taxes fall into two forms:

   a. _____ for _____

   b. _____ for _____

6. When people complain about taxes, they say that. . . .

   a. _____

   b. _____

   Americans generally agree _____.

C. Think About It

In the United States, as in many countries, the citizens do not enjoy paying taxes so collecting taxes can be a problem. The Swedish government has an interesting solution. Each year it publishes a book with a list of all individual taxpayers who earn the equivalent of $15,000 or more and each married couple who earns $20,000 or more. The book is similar to the telephone book. In this way, everyone knows how much money you make and how much you pay in taxes.

This system would not be useful in the United States. Americans are very private about many things, especially how much money they make. This would not be a good system of keeping track of taxes. Are salaries private in your country? Is it impolite to ask a person how much money he or she makes?

D. Reading

Running a government is very expensive. In the United States, most of the money comes from taxes—both from individuals and from corporations. Another part comes from social security payments (about 7 percent of an individual's salary). Other money comes from borrowing. But what happens to this money? Figure 1 indicates where the 1987–1988 budget came from and Figure 2, how the money was spent.

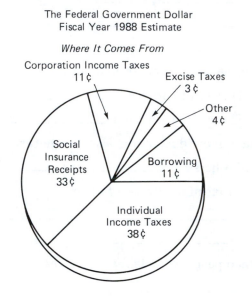

The Federal Government Dollar
Fiscal Year 1988 Estimate

Where It Comes From

Figure 1

1. What percentage of the U.S. budget comes from income taxes?

2. Who contributes more to the federal government—corporations or individuals?

3. How much of the federal budget comes from excise taxes?

4. What percentage comes from borrowing (taking money now and paying it back later)?

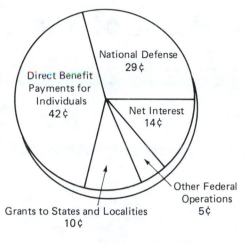

Figure 2

1. Where does the largest part of the federal budget go?

2. How much of the federal budget is used for the protection of the country?

3. How much support does the federal government give to states and cities or towns?

4. Which area does the president's salary come from?

5. What percentage of the federal budget supports retired people and people who are poor or have health problems?

Contact a Point of View

INCOME

A. Background Building

Figure 3 illustrates part of a page from the U.S. tax forms. Imagine that you are a single person who earns $26,125 in taxable income. What do you have to pay the federal government? Scan the table to find out. What percentage of your income is that figure?

If 1040A, line 17, OR 1040EZ, line 7 is—		And you are—				If 1040A, line 17, OR 1040EZ, line 7 is—		And you are—				If 1040A, line 17, OR 1040EZ, line 7 is—		And you are—			
At least	But less than	Single (and 1040EZ filers)	Married filing jointly	Married filing separately	Head of a household	At least	But less than	Single (and 1040EZ filers)	Married filing jointly	Married filing separately	Head of a household	At least	But less than	Single (and 1040EZ filers)	Married filing jointly	Married filing separately	Head of a household
		Your tax is—						Your tax is—						Your tax is—			
23,000						**26,000**						**29,000**					
23,000	23,050	4,191	3,334	4,604	3,357	26,000	26,050	5,031	3,784	5,654	4,197	29,000	29,050	6,013	4,367	6,704	5,037
23,050	23,100	4,205	3,341	4,621	3,371	26,050	26,100	5,045	3,791	5,671	4,211	29,050	29,100	6,030	4,381	6,721	5,051
23,100	23,150	4,219	3,349	4,639	3,385	26,100	26,150	5,059	3,799	5,689	4,225	29,100	29,150	6,048	4,395	6,739	5,065
23,150	23,200	4,233	3,356	4,656	3,399	26,150	26,200	5,073	3,806	5,706	4,239	29,150	29,200	6,065	4,409	6,756	5,079

Figure 3

B. Timed Reading

DIRECTIONS: *Read the following point of view and answer the questions in four minutes.*

Some people have all the luck. Here I am, a family man with three small children. I work hard for everything I have: a nice car, a house in the suburbs, and other conveniences. Lately on TV, I've seen groups of people on welfare who complain that they can't get by on their incomes. How do you think I feel? People on welfare never work and have seven or eight children. Who pays the bills? I do. About 25 percent of my salary goes to taxes: the federal and the state taxes. Then, of course, there is the property tax on the house and the excise tax on the car. I've had it with taxes. Besides, the rate of inflation is increasing daily. It really angers me that I can't have the kind of life I deserve—the kind of life that I have worked for.

The president says that these are hard times and that we should not spend so much money, and then the defense budget goes up. The local politicians say that they need more money for highway repairs, and then they vote a salary increase for themselves. The town selectmen say we need a new elementary school. We just can't afford it. Who helps me when the kids need new sneakers? No one. People used to say that the rich get richer and the poor get poorer. Now I am beginning to think that the people in the middle class are the real losers.

DIRECTIONS: *Read each of the following statements carefully to determine whether each is true (T), false (F), or impossible to know (ITK).*

1. _____ This man lives in the city.

2. _____ Twenty-five percent of his salary goes to taxes.

3. _____ He has three older children.

4. _____ He pays taxes on his home.

5. _____ Money for education comes from the state.

6. _____ He is on welfare.

7. _____ He is from the upper class.

8. _____ He thinks that the middle class is lucky.

9. _____ Local politicians have high salaries.

10. _____ The president wants people to conserve.

C. Vocabulary

DIRECTIONS: Circle the letter of the word(s) with the same meaning as the italicized word(s).

1. I can't have the kind of life I *deserve.*

   a. should have   b. can have   c. had

2. It *angers* him that he can't have an easy life.

   a. confuses   b. upsets   c. worries

3. We should not *complain* about taxes. They are necessary.

   a. feel unhappy   b. say bad things   c. care

4. The defense budget *goes up* yearly.

   a. decreases   b. increases   c. changes

5. These are some of our *local* politicians.

   a. far away   b. misplaced   c. from the area

6. A large percentage of the national budget is for *defense.*

   a. politicians   b. the military   c. the presidency

7. People in the middle class are the real *losers.*

   a. people who don't gain   b. people who don't lose   c. people who complain

8. There are many *conveniences* in American homes.

   a. interesting things   b. affordable objects   c. helpful things

D. React

DIRECTIONS: Work with a committee of three or four students and plan a budget for your country. Take the roles of the president, the minister of defense, the minister of human services, and the minister of transportation. Fill out the pie on page 195 to show how you would organize your budget. Be prepared to present your budget to the public (the other students in your class).

_____ defense	_____ health care
_____ welfare	_____ day-care centers
_____ unemployment compensation	_____ roads and highways
_____ social security	_____ public transportation
_____ education	_____ energy research
_____ old-age homes	_____ pollution control

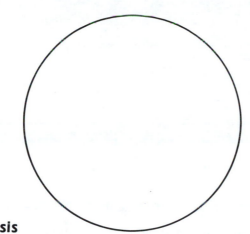

E. Word Analysis

DIRECTIONS: Read the following information about <u>adverbs</u> and <u>adjectives</u> and then complete the exercises. Decide if the italicized words in the sentences are adverbs or adjectives.

(noun)

<u>Adjectives</u> explain <u>nouns</u> more clearly. He is a <u>slow</u> speaker.

(verb)

<u>Adverbs</u> explain <u>verbs</u> more clearly: He speaks <u>slowly</u>.

<u>Adverbs</u> can also explain <u>adjectives</u> or other <u>adverbs</u> more clearly:

(adverb)   (adjective)

She speaks <u>very</u> slowly. She is a <u>very</u> slow speaker.

	ADVERB	ADJECTIVE
1. She is always *independent*.	_____	_____
2. His ideas are *practically* impossible.	_____	_____
3. She arrives late *consistently*.	_____	_____
4. Those cars are really *fast*.	_____	_____
5. He drives *fast*.	_____	_____
6. They are a *typical* American family.	_____	_____
7. I *always* get up late.	_____	_____
8. *Lately*, I have been thinking about a vacation.	_____	_____
9. The style of her letter was very *formal*.	_____	_____
10. *Naturally*, she doesn't want to give up her job.	_____	_____

Look Back

A. Vocabulary

DIRECTIONS: Circle the letter of the choice that best completes each sentence.

1. He has many strong ideas. He is very _____.

   a. opinionated   b. changeable   c. impractical

2. We cannot decide; we _____ about everything.

   a. raise   b. avoid   c. disagree

3. Food is not _____ in some states.

   a. graduated   b. taxable   c. variable

4. My watch is very _____.

   a. valuable   b. conflicting   c. solvable

5. He gave me the wrong directions. I was _____.

   a. impractical   b. misinformed   c. directed

6. My telephone bill is _____ tomorrow.

   a. paid   b. due   c. differentiated

7. She _____ happy, but I'm not sure.

   a. tends to be   b. certainly is   c. seems

8. He is a good father; he is very _____ his children.

   a. supportive of   b. dependent on   c. uncertain of

9. The federal government _____ many educational programs.

   a. consists of   b. funds   c. spends

10. The students were very dissatisfied. We listened to their _____.

   a. experiences   b. complaints   c. models

B. Matching

DIRECTIONS: *Find the word or phrase in column B which has a similar mean-*
ing to a word or phrase in column A. Write the letter of that
word or phrase next to the word or phrase in column A.

	A		B
1. _____	impractical	a.	property
2. _____	possessions	b.	complain
3. _____	seem to	c.	useless
4. _____	protest	d.	utilize
5. _____	comprise	e.	extra
6. _____	additional	f.	appear to
7. _____	national	g.	include
8. _____	kind	h.	federal
9. _____	repair	i.	type
10. _____	use	j.	fix

C. Synthesis Questions

1. Take a survey in your class about taxes in different countries. Compare the percentage of taxes in your country to those of your classmates' countries.

2. Go to the local library and ask for tax forms and information. These
are easy to get from January 1 until April 15, the due date for taxes.
Look up the tax payment for someone who earns $40,000 taxable in-
come; what percent is it?

3. In some countries, taxes are high, but the government sponsors many
programs for its citizens, such as free medical assistance or public
education through the university level. What does your government
do with tax money? Do you think that there could be other ways of
spending your tax money?

D. Vocabulary Preview

DIRECTIONS: *What shorter words can you see in these words from Chapter 12?*

official	(1) _____		basic	(6) _____
resultant	(2) _____		Protestant	(7) _____
representation	(3) _____		existence	(8) _____
breakthrough	(4) _____ _____		de-emphasize	(9) _____
intermarriage	(5) _____		community	(10) _____

Freedom of Religion

A First Look

A. Background Building

1. What religions are represented in the illustration on the preceding page?

2. Do you know anyone who is a member of these religions?

3. What religions are most common in the U.S.? How about in your country?

4. Before you read, decide if the following statements are true (T) or false (F). Discuss your answers with your classmates.

1. _____ Every country should have a national religion.

2. _____ Everyone in the United States is a Christian.

3. _____ Roman Catholics are Christians.

4. _____ Protestants are Christians.

5. _____ Jews believe in God.

6. _____ The majority of people in the United States are Protestants and Jews.

7. _____ President John F. Kennedy was Roman Catholic.

8. _____ Two people of different religions cannot get married in the United States.

9. _____ Natives of a country should share a religion.

10. _____ People never have trouble in the United States because of their religion.

B. Topic

DIRECTIONS: *Before you begin to read, look at these topics. There is one topic for each paragraph. Look quickly at the reading to find these topics. Do not read every word at this point. Write the number of the paragraph next to the topic of that paragraph.*

1. _____ general description of Christianity

2. _____ the Jewish religion

3. _____ the Protestant church

4. _____ historical background for freedom of religion

5. _____ the Roman Catholic church

6. _____ traditional feelings about non-Protestant beliefs

7. _____ de-emphasis on religion

C. Reading

DIRECTIONS: Now read.

1   The first immigrants who came to New England in the 1600s   *1*
left their own countries for religious reasons. They had religious   *2*
beliefs different from the accepted beliefs of their country; they   *3*
wanted to live in a place where they could be free to have their own   *4*
beliefs. When they came to establish new communities in the New   *5*
World, they decided that there would be no official religion. When   *6*
this new country gained its independence from Britain in 1776, the   *7*
separation of church and state was one of the basic laws for the   *8*
United States. This absence of an official national religion and the   *9*
resultant freedom to believe in whatever one wants has attracted   *10*
many new immigrants. In the United States, there are examples of   *11*
every kind of world religion—Buddhist, Islamic, Baha'i, to name   *12*
only a few. Many religions also began in the United States such as the   *13*
Pentecostals, Mormons and Christian Science religions. But most of the   *14*
people in the United States fall into one of two categories—Christian   *15*
or Jewish.   *16*

2   The majority of people in the United States were raised as   *17*
Christians. Quite simply, Christian means believing in Christ, or Je-   *18*
sus. Christians celebrate Christmas, the birth of Christ, and Easter,   *19*
the time at which Christians remember Jesus's death and celebrate   *20*
His rebirth. They think of Sunday as a holy day and worship in   *21*
churches. In the United States, Christianity can be divided into two   *22*
major groups: Roman Catholicism and Protestantism. A third   *23*
group, Orthodoxy, is not as common in the United States.   *24*

3   As its name suggests, the Roman Catholic church is based in   *25*
Rome. It is centered around the authority of one man, the Pope,   *26*
who is the head of the Roman Catholic church throughout the world.   *27*
There is a hierarchy of authority and responsibility beginning with   *28*
the Pope in Rome and ending with the priests who are the heads of   *29*
the churches in individual neighborhoods and communities.   *30*

As its name suggests, the Protestant church began as a pro-   *31*
test against another church: the Roman Catholic church. Protes-   *32*

tant is a very general term; it includes many different church *33*
groups, such as Episcopalian, Presbyterian, Lutheran, Methodist, *34*

4   Baptist, and many more. The majority of people in the United States *35*
have Protestant backgrounds. However, since there are so many *36*
Protestant churches, each with its own traditions, people who are *37*
Protestants do not really share similar religious experiences. As op- *38*
posed to the Roman Catholic church in which there is a lot of central *39*
control, Protestant churches are generally more autonomous, with *40*
more control and authority on a local level. *41*

    Jews and Christians share many of the same basic principles *42*
and beliefs. They both believe in the existence of one God. But *43*
whereas Christians believe in Christ, a representation of God on *44*
earth, Jews do not believe that God has come to earth in any form. *45*

5   Jewish people celebrate a weekly holy day from Friday evening to *46*
Saturday evening and worship in synagogues. The head of a syn- *47*
agogue is called a rabbi. Many Jewish people came to the United *48*
States in the first half of the twentieth century because of religious *49*
intolerance in their own countries. *50*

    Although freedom of religion is an important concept in the *51*
United States, religious intolerance sometimes occurs. Because the *52*
majority of early Americans were Protestant, there has sometimes *53*
been discrimination against new immigrants, such as the Irish and *54*

6   Italians, who were Roman Catholic. Protestants were reluctant to *55*
share their traditional power with members of other churches or *56*
religions. The year 1960 marked a breakthrough in the religious tol- *57*
erance of the country when John F. Kennedy, a Roman Catholic, *58*
became the first non-Protestant President of the United States. *59*

    The second half of the twentieth century has seen a decline in *60*
the strength of traditional religion in the United States. It is prob- *61*

7   ably to be expected that in a society that accepts so many different *62*
religions, religion would be de-emphasized. Intermarriage is now *63*
common and fewer people think about traditional religious beliefs. *64*

React

Find some information in the reading that surprised you.
Discuss it with your classmates.

D. Scanning/Vocabulary

DIRECTIONS: Find a synonym for the word given in the paragraph indicated.

Paragraph 1

1. traditional   _____

2. build   _____

3. sactioned by government   _____

4. division   _____

5. essential   _____

6. lack   _____

7. interested   _____

Paragraph 2

8. greatest number   _____

9. brought up   _____

Paragraph 3

10. power and control   _____

11. leader   _____

12. power structure   _____

E. Reading Comprehension

DIRECTIONS: Circle the letter of the choice that best completes each sentence.

1. Most people in the United States have _____ backgrounds.

   a. Protestant   b. Roman Catholic   c. Jewish

2. The early Americans were _____.

   a. Protestant   b. Roman Catholic   c. Jewish

3. Many Jewish people came to the United States _____.

   a. in the 1600s   b. before 1950   c. in the 1950s

4. According to the author, _____ is more hierarchical than other religions.

   a. the Jewish religion   b. Protestantism   c. Roman Catholicism

5. According to the author, in the second half of the twentieth century, traditional religion has _____ power.

   a. gained   b. lost   c. no

6. According to the author, there _____ religious discrimination in the United States.

   a. is now no   b. has sometimes been   c. never used to be

7. Protestants belong to _____.

   a. many different   b. the Roman Catholic   c. similar churches
       churches   church

8. The United States has _____ religion.

   a. an official   b. no   c. no official

9. The _____ people came to the United States because of religious freedom.

   a. Jewish   b. Irish   c. Buddhist

10. In the Protestant church, there is _____ control on the local level.

   a. no   b. a lot of   c. rarely

Look Again

A. Vocabulary

DIRECTIONS: Circle the letter of the choice that best completes each sentence.

1. Both churches and synagogues are places where people ____.

   a. believe   b. worship   c. attract

2. Most large organizations have a ____ of power and authority.

   a. hierarchy   b. reluctance   c. reason

3. My friend is the ____ of the department. She is the supervisor.

   a. head   b. representation   c. priest

4. A director in a company has the ____ to make decisions.

   a. hierarchy   b. persecution   c. authority

5. This painting is an example of realism. It is a ____ of a rainstorm.

   a. concept   b. representation   c. principle

6. He never thinks about his religious ____.

   a. level   b. head   c. beliefs

7. The mayor of a city is not involved in the federal government. The mayor is in ____ government.

   a. national   b. individual   c. local

8. The president's wife was the ____ head of the company.

   a. unofficial   b. attracted   c. raised

9. The town, not the state, had control of its own policies. The town was ____.

   a. autonomous   b. tolerant   c. centered

10. We decided not to go running ____ it was raining out.

   a. throughout   b. since   c. as opposed to

B. Reading Comprehension

DIRECTIONS: Complete the outline of the reading.

I. Introduction

_____

_____

II. _____

_____

_____

_____

III. _____

_____

_____

IV. _____

_____

_____

V. _____

_____

_____

VI. _____

_____

_____

VII. _____

_____

_____

C. Think About It

DIRECTIONS: Answer the following questions.

1. Does your country have an official religion?
2. Do you know of any official religions of countries of the world?

3. What are the countries and the religions?

4. Work with your classmates to complete this chart. List any religions.

	RELIGION 1	RELIGION 2	RELIGION 3	RELIGION 4
Name	_____	_____	_____	_____
Religious Leaders	_____	_____	_____	_____
Special Building(s)	_____	_____	_____	_____
Book(s)	_____	_____	_____	_____
Holidays/ Celebrations	_____	_____	_____	_____
Rules	_____	_____	_____	_____
	_____	_____	_____	_____
Beliefs	_____	_____	_____	_____
	_____	_____	_____	_____

D. Reading

DIRECTIONS: Study the information in the graph and answer the following questions.

Religious Preference in the United States
(in percentage)

YEAR	PROTESTANT	CATHOLIC	JEWISH	OTHER	NONE
1957	66	26	3	1	3
1967	67	25	3	3	2
1975	62	27	2	4	6
1980	61	28	2	2	7
1985	57	28	2	4	9

1. Which religion do the majority of people prefer?

2. Has religion become more popular or less? How do you know?

3. Which religious groups have grown in popularity since 1957?

4. Are you surprised by these numbers? If so, what surprises you?

Contact a Point of View

A. Background Building

DIRECTIONS: Answer the following questions.

1. Are you very religious? Do you pray or go to church/mosque/temple/synagogue? How often?

2. Do your parents and family have the same religious beliefs as you do?

B. Timed Reading

Kathy Robinson is a very religious person. She feels that her relationship with God is the most important thing in her life. Her closest friends are also very devout and they meet once a week to pray together and to talk about their religious beliefs and experiences.

Kathy is a management trainee at a large bank. When she went to work at the bank last year, she met an interesting man, Bob Thomas. Everyone in Kathy's department thought Bob was amazing because he became a top manager so quickly. Kathy liked him because he was kind to the management trainees and was always available to help them with questions and problems. After Kathy had been at the bank three months, Bob left Kathy's bank to become a vice-president at another bank. Everyone was sorry to see him leave.

When Bob started his new job, he called Kathy and invited her to lunch. Soon they were going out for dinner and movies as well. They had a lot in common and Kathy soon realized that Bob was in love with her. She also feels very strongly about him, but there is one problem. Bob is not a religious person. He never prays or even thinks about God. Bob wants to marry Kathy but Kathy, even though she loves Bob too, thinks that she should stop seeing him.

DIRECTIONS: Read each of the following statements carefully to determine whether each is true (T), false (F), or impossible to know (ITK).

1. _____ Kathy's closest friends are very religious people.

2. _____ Kathy and Bob work at the same bank.

3. _____ Kathy and Bob have known each other for three years.

4. _____ Bob was successful at Kathy's bank.

5. _____ Kathy is a manager in the bank.

6. _____ Kathy and Bob share a lot of interests.

7. _____ Kathy's friends think she should stop seeing Bob.

8. _____ Her religious beliefs are more important than marriage to Kathy.

9. _____ Bob did not ask Kathy out when they worked together.

10. _____ Kathy wants to marry someone who shares her religious beliefs.

C. Vocabulary

DIRECTIONS: Circle the letter of the word(s) with the same meaning as the italicized word.

1. They are *devout* Christians.

   a. serious   b. very religious   c. unhappy

2. We are *praying* that he will recover from his injuries.

   a. asking God   b. trying to help   c. believing in God

3. This is *amazing* news!

   a. serious   b. interesting   c. surprising

4. We don't have much *in common.*

   a. normally   b. typically   c. of shared interest

5. I'll be *available* between 10 and 12 o'clock in my office.

   a. willing to help you   b. able to go out   c. busy working

6. I don't discuss my *beliefs* very often.

   a. thoughts   b. things I think are true   c. what society is convinced of

7. Which *department* do you work in?

   a. division of a company   b. field of work   c. government office

8. Becky and Karl are *seeing* each other.

   a. watching   b. visiting   c. going out with

9. I didn't *realize* how you felt about this.

   a. understand   b. think   c. remember

10. They are enrolled in a computer *training* program.

   a. instruction   b. design   c. teaching

D. React

DIRECTIONS: Discuss the following questions with your classmates.

1. How important is it to marry someone who shares your feelings about religion? Why?

2. If Kathy and Bob get married, what problems might they face?

3. What do you think they should do?

4. Bob didn't ask Kathy out until he was working at a different bank. Perhaps the bank had a rule against dating or marrying someone you work with. Is this rule common in your country?

E. Word Analysis

DIRECTIONS: *Choose the appropriate word form for each sentence. Is it an adjective or an adverb?*

ADJECTIVE	ADVERB
natural	naturally
formal	formally

1. careful
   carefully

2. traditional
   traditionally

3. essential
   essentially

4. serious
   seriously

5. perfect
   perfectly

6. social
   socially

7. cultural
   culturally

8. vast
   vastly

9. minimal
   minimally

10. ironic
    ironically

1. He spoke _____ about the problem.

2. My father dresses very _____.

3. It is _____ to study all aspects of the problem.

4. She is _____ about her work.

5. That design is _____ beautiful.

6. He is nervous _____.

7. Lifestyles vary _____.

8. Our opinions are _____ different.

9. That change is _____.

10. That play was extremely _____.

Look Back

A. Vocabulary

DIRECTIONS: Circle the letter of the choice that best completes each sentence.

1. I don't know very much about his _____, but his present behavior is more important to me.

   a. autonomy   b. background   c. authority

2. The biggest part of a group of people is the _____.

   a. minority   b. majority   c. population

3. What is the _____ for the marriage between two religions or races?

   a. term   b. intermarriage   c. portion

4. There wasn't any sugar _____, so I used honey.

   a. seeing   b. autonomous   c. available

5. I use a yellow pen to _____ the important sentences in the book.

   a. experience   b. emphasize   c. breakthrough

6. My _____ idea is the same as yours; we just disagree about the details.

   a. unsuccessful   b. local   c. basic

7. There is no _____ between the different living areas of the house. It is all one big room.

   a. discrimination   b. separation   c. independence

8. Which church do you _____ in?

   a. worship   b. head   c. occur

9. The discovery of electricity was a great _____.

   a. breakthrough   b. belief   c. reference

10. How much money do you need to _____ a business?

    a. see   b. discriminate   c. establish

B. Matching

DIRECTIONS: Find the word or phrase in column B which has a similar meaning to a word in column A. Write the letter of that word or
phrase next to the word in Column A.

	A		B
1.	_____ tolerance	a.	idea
2.	_____ decline	b.	someone learning in a business
3.	_____ occur	c.	acceptance
4.	_____ separation	d.	because
5.	_____ concept	e.	self-government
6.	_____ belief	f.	word
7.	_____ local	g.	decrease
8.	_____ term	h.	happen
9.	_____ trainee	i.	principle
10.	_____ since	j.	split
11.	_____ autonomy	k.	near

C. Synthesis Questions

1. Do you feel that religion affects everyday life? If so, how?

2. Is religion becoming more or less important in your country?

3. Interview someone from one of the religions you have discussed or read about in this chapter. Work with your classmates to develop interview questions.

A Changing America

A. Background Building

DIRECTIONS: Think for a few minutes about what aspects of American life you have read about and discussed in this book. Write down as many concepts as you can:

_____

_____

_____

B. Reading

DIRECTIONS: Now read.

1   The United States is similar to most other countries in the world. *1*
Like other countries, the U.S. is changing at a very fast pace. Our values *2*
and our people are changing, and many people are afraid of these changes. *3*

2   The 1950s was the last decade of calm for this country. The fifties *4*
was a time of convertibles, poodle skirts and hula hoops. It was a prob- *5*
lem free time when life was predictable and you had no fear of leaving *6*
your door unlocked. Since that time there have been many changes in *7*
the country. The American population is changing. There are now many *8*
more Asian Americans and Hispanics than ever before. Americans are *9*
getting older and the number of senior citizens continues to increase. *10*
Because of birth control, the high cost of raising children, and perhaps *11*
because of uncertainty about the future, we are having fewer babies. *12*

3   Americans are moving, too. They are going to the warmer parts of *13*
the country, to some of the older cities, and to some large suburban areas. *14*
When they move, they often leave their home towns and extended fam- *15*
ilies behind. They have to create new friends wherever they go. Some- *16*
times, the office becomes the new neighborhood and people at the office *17*
become our friends and "neighbors." *18*

4   We are a wealthy country, but our wealth is not evenly distributed. *19*
We still have homeless people, hungry children, and crime. Some immi- *20*
grants have the idea that "the streets are paved with gold." Hard work *21*
still brings great results, as evidenced by the newest immigrants, but *22*
unemployment is a problem in many parts of the country. For some *23*
Americans, the United States is not a land of opportunities. *24*

5   American women are working more, but still do not have the same *25*
opportunities for equal salaries and advancement as men. They often find *26*
that they have two jobs now: taking care of the house and the children *27*
as well as working at the office. *28*

6   Racial discrimination is illegal; every American citizen is guaran- *29*
teed equal opportunity before the law, but prejudice and fear of other *30*
groups still persist. Blacks continue to earn less than whites throughout *31*

the work force, and certain cities have become almost totally black be-   32
cause of the movement of whites to the suburbs. These forms of discrim-   33
ination and segregation are almost impossible to control.   34

    Government decisions in Washington greatly affect individuals.   35
Some 30 percent of our tax money is being used for defense and less   36
and less used for social programs. Religion is still a private issue, but   37
there are many areas such as school prayer and abortion where the gov-   38
ernment is making decisions about private, ethical matters.   39

    Americans worry about the same issues as other people around the   40
world, about their children, and how their lives will be. They worry about   41
nuclear war, about international terrorism, and about too much govern-   42
ment control. They know that this time is a period of immense change,   43
but they also realize that change can be beneficial even if it is difficult.   44
They face many uncertainties, but perhaps the pioneer spirit which built   45
the country will also help Americans change, improve, and adapt to the   46
future.

7

8

React

Look at your list from Exercise A and see how it compares to the article. Did you write down any concepts
which the author did not mention? Did the author mention any ideas which you did not think of?

C. Vocabulary

*DIRECTIONS: Find each of the following words in the reading and write the
line number where you found it. Then write a word with a
similar meaning on the line.*

1. pace   ____   _____

2. afraid   ____   _____

3. calm   ____   _____

4. predictable   ____   _____

5. uncertainty   ____   _____

6. extended   ____   _____

7. create   ____   _____

8. distributed   ____   _____

9. homeless   _____   _____

10. evidenced   _____   _____

11. worry   _____   _____

12. nuclear   _____   _____

13. terrorism   _____   _____

14. immense   _____   _____

15. realize   _____   _____

D. Word Forms: Review

DIRECTIONS: *Choose the appropriate word form for each sentence. Is it a noun, adjective, adverb, or verb?*

general
generally
generalize
generalization

individual
individually
individualize
individualization

differ
different
differently
difference

free
freely
freedom

simple
simply
simplify
simplification

1. We _____ go home at about 5:30 P.M.

2. It is easy to _____ about things which are unfamiliar to you.

3. The teacher talked to each student _____.

4. Your _____ opinion is important to me.

5. We do things very _____.

6. What _____ does it make?

7. May I speak _____?

8. You are _____ to do whatever you want.

9. I know a _____ solution to the problem.

10. I think that I need to _____ my life.

E. Synthesis Questions

1. Many of the issues mentioned in this concluding reading concern problems in the United States, but similar problems exist throughout

the world. Choose one issue which you have read about and discuss it in relationship to your own country.

2. All important issues in life are complex. Choose another one of the issues discussed in this book and take the sides of the various people involved. Role play and figure out how to solve the problem. For example, a husband and wife and the issues of working, taking care of the house and the children; a senior citizen who wants more help from the government and a government official; or an Asian American parent who must send his or her six-year-old child to a school in another part of the city and the principal of the elementary school.